AUSTRALIAN SLANG & IDIOMS

THE FUN DICTIONARY OF AUSSIE EXPRESSIONS &
SAYINGS TO SPEAK LIKE A LOCAL

LILY KOALA

Copyright © 2025 Lily Koala

All rights reserved. No part of this publication may be reproduced, distributed, or transmitted in any form or by any means, including photocopying, recording, or other electronic or mechanical methods, without the prior written permission of the publisher, except in the case of brief quotations embodied in critical reviews and certain other non-commercial uses permitted by copyright law.

Trademarked names appear throughout this book. Rather than use a trademark symbol with every occurrence of a trademarked name, names are used in an editorial fashion, with no intention of infringement of the respective owner's trademark. The information in this book is distributed on an "as is" basis, without warranty. Although every precaution has been taken in the preparation of this work, neither the author nor the publisher shall have any liability to any person or entity with respect to any loss or damage caused or alleged to be caused directly or indirectly by the information contained in this book.

CONTENTS

Introduction   v
A Brief History   vii

A	1
B	9
C	29
D	42
E	50
F	53
G	59
H	65
I	70
J	73
K	76
L	80
M	83
N	88
O	91
P	95
Q	101
R	103
S	108
T	114
U	119
V	121
W	123
X	128
Y	129
Z	132
Stories Behind the Slang	134

Conclusion   147
Thanks for Reading!   149

INTRODUCTION

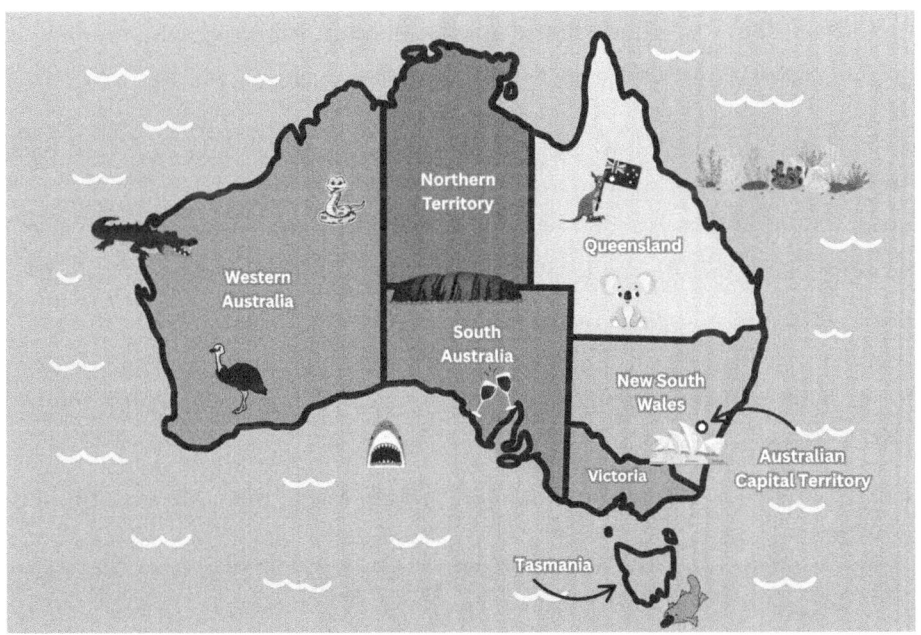

G'day, mates! Welcome to *Australian Slang & Idioms*.

This book is your step-by-step guide for learning how Australians really speak. Forget the stiff classroom English you might find in textbooks. Aussie slang is casual, quick, and packed with personality. It's how people actually chat in pubs, on beaches, at work, and in the middle of a good laugh with friends.

Why bother learning slang? Simple — it helps you blend in, connect faster, and dodge those awkward moments when someone says, "Catch ya later," and you start looking around wondering who's throwing what at you. Slang is more than just words; it's part of daily life.

Inside this book, you'll find:

- Words and Phrases — The most common slang terms you'll hear across Australia.
- Clear Definitions — No long explanations, just straight-to-the-point meanings.
- How to Use Them — Simple examples so you can drop the phrases into real conversations.
- Quick Tips — Handy notes about whether a word is casual, funny, or best kept for mates instead of the boss.

You can use this book however it suits you. Flip through it at your own pace and look up words as you go, or set yourself a goal to learn a few new terms every day until they become second nature. Either way, you'll always have a clear guide to help you sound natural.

So, grab a cuppa, take it one word at a time, and enjoy learning the slang that makes Aussie English unique. By the time you're done, you'll know how to throw in a "G'day," laugh at a "good yarn," and sign off with a relaxed "No worries."

Fair go, mate — you're about to sound more Aussie than you ever thought possible.

A BRIEF HISTORY

Australia's story is as unique as its slang. For more than 60,000 years, Aboriginal and Torres Strait Islander peoples have lived on this land, developing one of the world's oldest continuous cultures. Their lives were deeply tied to Country (the land, waters, and skies) and their languages, stories, and traditions carried knowledge across countless generations. That connection still shapes modern Australia today, from Dreamtime stories and bush medicine to art and songlines that describe both history and geography.

Everything changed in 1788, when the First Fleet of British ships arrived in Sydney Cove. What began as a penal colony (a dumping ground for convicts) was harsh and unforgiving. Life was tough, food was scarce, and the climate was unlike anything the settlers had known. But from those beginnings grew a nation marked by resilience, grit, and a talent for finding humour in the hardest circumstances. Aussies still celebrate that underdog spirit, and it shows in how they speak: slang is often blunt, witty, and built to cut through pretension.

As the colony expanded, gold rushes in the 1850s brought migrants from across the globe; not only more Europeans but also thousands of Chinese miners and merchants. Later waves of migration after World War II welcomed Italians, Greeks, Vietnamese, and many others. Each community added new flavours to the culture — from food to festivals to language. Australia today is a vibrant mix, where you can grab a meat pie, a kebab, or pho on the same street. That multicultural influence filters into the way people talk, blending old British turns of phrase with new twists and local flavour.

By 1901, the colonies had federated into one nation: the Commonwealth of Australia. Aussies built their identity on a few key values — mateship, sticking by your friends no matter what; a fair go, the idea that everyone deserves a chance; and not taking yourself too seriously, which is why the language is filled with cheeky insults that somehow sound affectionate.

Aussie English also carries its own quirks. People often call things "she" — especially cars, boats, or machines. It's not about gender, just a playful way of talking. Saying, "She won't start" about a ute, or "She'll be right" about a problem, is part of the Aussie way of giving personality to things. Another twist is the habit of ending sentences with "as" for emphasis, without finishing the comparison. For example: "Can't come to work today, feel crook as," texted Sharon. It simply means *really crook* — no need to add anything more.

These playful quirks aren't the only thing shaping Aussie slang. The landscape itself shaped the lingo, too. The vast outback gave rise to colourful expressions, while the beach lifestyle gave Australians their easygoing, sun-soaked vocabulary. Words like *bush telegraph*, *stubbie*, or *barbie* grew naturally out of the way people lived. Even the tendency to shorten words — from "arvo" for afternoon to "Woolies" for Woolworths — comes from that laid-back, time-saving style.

So when you pick up a phrase like "no worries," "a cold one," or "fair dinkum," you're not just learning slang. You're catching a glimpse of a whole way of life. Aussie English is part history lesson, part cultural handshake, and part invitation to laugh along. From the city pub to the backyard barbecue, from the beaches of Bondi to the red dirt of the outback, slang is one of the truest reflections of how Australians see themselves: practical, funny, and always ready to connect.

A

A Cold One

Definition: A cold beer.

How to Use It: After a long day working under the hot sun, Mick kicked off his boots and said, "Time for a cold one!" His friends laughed as they cracked open their beers, knowing nothing beats the first sip after a hard day's work. The phrase "a cold one" is one of the most common Aussie ways to ask for a beer, often linked with friendship, relaxation, and winding down.

Ace

Definition: Fantastic; very good.

How to Use It: After winning the local football match, Josh grinned and said, "That last goal was ace!" His mates cheered and slapped him on the back, knowing it was the play that had turned the game. The word "ace" highlights moments of success, skill, or excitement, and is often used to celebrate something truly impressive.

Advert

Definition: Short for advertisement.

How to Use It: While waiting for the train, Kylie pointed at the billboard and said, "Have you seen that new car advert? Looks pretty slick." Her friend nodded, recalling how Aussies casually shorten words whenever possible. The term "advert" is just another example of this Aussie tendency to keep language short, sharp, and easy.

Aerial Ping Pong

Definition: A somewhat derogatory way of referring to Australian Rules Football (AFL).

How to Use It: At the pub, someone laughed and said, "You still watching that aerial ping pong every weekend?" The room chuckled as the AFL fan rolled his eyes, used to the joke from his rugby friends. The phrase pokes fun at the game's high kicks and fast pace, showing the playful rivalry between sports.

Tip: This phrase can be insulting depending on tone.

Aggro

Definition: Aggressive or filled with aggression.

How to Use It: During the match, tensions rose, and one fan turned aggro, yelling at the umpire until security stepped in. His friends shook their heads, knowing alcohol had played a part. The word often paints a picture of someone losing control, especially in heated social or sporting situations.

Airy-Fairy

Definition: Vague, unclear, or nonsensical.

How to Use It: Jess asked for directions, but the man's response was so airy-fairy that she ended up more lost than before. Later, she laughed about it, realising she'd travelled in circles. The phrase "airy-fairy" describes explanations or plans that sound fanciful but lack any real substance.

Akubra

Definition: A well-known brand of wide-brimmed Australian hats, often linked with farmers and the outback.

How to Use It: Sarah spotted her uncle at the country show and laughed, "Nice Akubra! Looks like you've come straight from the bush." Her uncle tipped the brim proudly, explaining that it had been with him through years of farm work and long days under the blazing sun. The "Akubra" is more than headwear — it's a trusted companion and a symbol of resilience in the Australian outdoors.

All Ears

Definition: To listen closely and give full attention.

How to Use It: When Luke said he had a new plan to save money on fuel, his friend replied, "I'm all ears, mate." He leaned forward, ready for every detail, showing he was giving his full attention. The phrase "all ears" goes beyond just listening — it signals interest, respect, and a willingness to hear someone out.

All Smiles

Definition: To stay cheerful and pleasant, even during tough times.

How to Use It: Despite her team losing the netball final, Emma was all smiles as she congratulated the winners. Her upbeat spirit lifted the mood around her. The phrase "all smiles" reflects the Aussie habit of staying positive and showing resilience, even when things don't go your way.

All the Go

Definition: Something very popular or trendy at the moment.

How to Use It: "That new burger place in town is all the go," Mark said as he joined the queue stretching around the corner. Everyone in town seemed to be talking about it. The phrase "all the go" is used when something is the current craze, often among young people or locals.

Amber Fluid

Definition: Beer, often referred to because of its amber colour.

How to Use It: After mowing the lawn on a hot summer day, Paul sat on the porch and said, "Time for some amber fluid." His neighbour soon joined him with a stubby in hand. The phrase "amber fluid" is a playful, old-fashioned way Aussies talk about beer, usually in casual settings.

Ambo

Definition: Short for ambulance or paramedic.

How to Use It: When a footy player collapsed on the field, the crowd gasped, and someone shouted, "Call an ambo!" Within minutes, the paramedics rushed in. The word "ambo" is everyday slang, reflecting how Aussies shorten words for convenience, even in serious situations.

Ankle Biter

Definition: A small child, often used jokingly or sometimes as a complaint.

How to Use It: During the family barbecue, Tom rolled his eyes and remarked, "The ankle biters are running wild today." The phrase is a light-hearted slang for kids, usually cheeky or noisy, though it can come across as rude if used with strangers.

Tip: The phrase is informal, and may seem impolite depending on context.

Anchors

Definition: Slang for brakes on a car or vehicle.

How to Use It: Driving down the steep hill, Lisa yelled, "Hit the anchors!" just before her friend slowed the car. In Aussie slang, "anchors" means brakes and is often used when talking about stopping quickly, especially in high-pressure or sudden situations.

Ant's Pants

Definition: Something excellent or of very high quality.

How to Use It: After tasting the new bakery's croissants, Mia smiled and said, "These are the ant's pants!" The phrase "ant's pants" is used to describe something top-notch or the best of its kind, often in food, fashion, or entertainment.

Arse About

Definition: To do something the wrong way or in a confused manner.

How to Use It: Tom tried fixing the shelves but put them upside down, and his friend groaned, "You've done it all arse about." The phrase "arse about" is used when something has been done completely backwards or wrong.

Arse Into Gear

Definition: To step it up, to stop lazing around, and get moving.

How to Use It: After an hour of watching TV instead of mowing the lawn, Jake's dad yelled, "Get your arse into gear, mate!" It's often used to push someone into action, especially when a job needs to be finished quickly.

Tip: Informal. Usually said in frustration but also in good humour.

Arsey

Definition: Slang for someone rude or unpleasant. A short form of arsehole.

How to Use It: When Kelly asked her brother for a lift and he refused without reason, she muttered, "You're being arsey today." The word is often used to call out behaviour that feels selfish or unfriendly.

Tip: Rude. Use only with close mates who won't take offence.

Arvo

Definition: Short for afternoon.

How to Use It: "Let's grab a coffee this arvo," Jess texted her friend. In Australia, "arvo" is one of the most common word shortenings, used daily in workplaces, schools, and with friends. Aussies love to shorten words, and "arvo" perfectly reflects that laid-back, time-saving style. It's rarely used in formal settings, but in casual plans or friendly chats, it's as natural as saying "afternoon."

Tip: Not to be confused with "avo," which means avocado.

As Cross as a Frog in a Sock

Definition: Very angry or upset.

How to Use It: After his car broke down again, Dave stormed into the workshop, as cross as a frog in a sock. He paced back and forth, muttering under his breath while the mechanic tried not to laugh at his temper. The expression is one of Australia's most colourful ways to describe anger, showing someone so wound up they can't sit still — just like a frog thrashing inside a sock.

At the Drop of a Hat

Definition: Very quickly or without hesitation.

How to Use It: When asked if she'd join the road trip, Lisa replied, "I'd pack and leave at the drop of a hat." Her mates laughed, knowing she was always ready for an adventure with no second thoughts. The phrase "at the drop of a hat" is often used to show eagerness or quick decision-making, reflecting a carefree or spontaneous attitude — the kind of Aussie spirit that says yes first and worries later.

Aussie

Definition: Refers to anything Australian. Pronounced "Ozzie."

How to Use It: Walking through the festival, Pete said, "This barbecue is as Aussie as it gets." The word is used proudly by locals and describes people, culture, or things tied to Australia.

Tip: Always pronounced with a "z" sound, never with an "s."

Aussie Salute

Definition: Waving a hand to swat away flies.

How to Use It: Camping in the Outback, Sarah kept giving the Aussie salute as flies buzzed around her face. The phrase humorously describes the constant battle against insects in hot parts of Australia.

Avo

Definition: Short for avocado.

How to Use It: At brunch, Mia sighed, "I'd love smashed avo, but it's twenty bucks a plate." The word "avo" is commonly heard in cafes, markets, and casual food chats, often tied to Australia's café culture. It's especially famous thanks to the "smashed avo on toast" debate, where older generations joked that millennials couldn't buy houses because they spent their savings on fancy avocado breakfasts.

Tip: Do not confuse with "arvo," which means afternoon.

Awning over the Toy Shop

Definition: A beer belly; the "awning" is the gut hanging over the "toy shop."

How to Use It: At the beach, Ben teased his mate, "You've got an awning over the toy shop — those swimmers don't hide much!" The phrase is cheeky slang for a rounded stomach, often caused by years of drinking.

Tip: Humorous but can be offensive if used the wrong way.

B

B & S

Definition: A rowdy country party for bachelors and spinsters (singles), often held in rural Australia. Once formal, these gatherings are now known for loud music, heavy drinking, and wild antics.

How to Use It: Tom packed his swag and said, "Heading out to the B & S this weekend, mate — heard it'll be massive." For many young Aussies in the bush, a B & S is a rite of passage: a chance to party hard, meet people, and blow off steam in the middle of nowhere.

Tip: Informal. Strongly linked to rural culture.

Backhander

Definition: A bribe, often money slipped quietly to avoid trouble.

How to Use It: After being pulled over for speeding, Shane muttered, "Nearly had to give the bloke a backhander to get out of that fine." The term "backhander" shows how Aussies describe shady under-the-table dealings.

Tip: Informal. Usually negative, suggests dishonesty.

Back of Beyond

Definition: A place so remote that it feels almost non-existent.

How to Use It: Driving through the outback, Jess laughed, "We're really in the back of beyond now — no fuel, no phone signal, just kangaroos." The phrase highlights Australia's vast, isolated regions, and is often used half-jokingly to describe anywhere far from civilisation.

Bad Trot

Definition: A stretch of bad luck or poor performance.

How to Use It: After losing three bets in a row, Rob shook his head and said, "On a bad trot, can't win a thing this week." The phrase "bad trot" is common in sport, gambling, or day-to-day struggles, showing how Aussies downplay misfortune with humour.

Bail Out

Definition: To leave a situation abruptly, or to help someone out of trouble.

How to Use It: After the pub argument got heated, Sarah decided to bail out before things turned nasty. The phrase "bail out" can mean escaping drama or stepping in to rescue a friend from a sticky spot.

Balls Up

Definition: A situation that has gone wrong or failed completely.

How to Use It: After the catering didn't arrive for the wedding, Rachel sighed, "This whole day's turned into a balls up." Aussies often use the phrase to describe a plan gone wrong — from sporting disasters to everyday mishaps.

Tip: Informal. It can be blunt or crude depending on the audience.

Banana Bender

Definition: A nickname for someone from Queensland, based on the state's banana farming.

How to Use It: Meeting someone at uni, Tom asked, "You're from Brissy? Ah, a banana bender then!" The phrase is used jokingly for Queenslanders, showing the Aussie love of state-based nicknames and playful rivalry.

Tip: Usually light-hearted, but can offend if used harshly.

Barbie

Definition: Aussie slang for a barbecue, one of the most beloved social events in the country. It's where friends gather, food sizzles, and the esky is full.

How to Use It: "We're firing up the barbie this arvo — bring some snags and a slab," said Sam. A barbie isn't just about cooking; it's about connection. From backyard gatherings to beach setups, it's where Aussies bond over food, beer, and banter.

Basket Case

Definition: Someone whose life is a mess or who can't cope; often used for people under stress or struggling.

How to Use It: After weeks of working double shifts, Jenny turned up exhausted and muttered, "I'm a basket case at this point." The phrase "basket case" is often used with a mix of sympathy and humour.

Bathers

Definition: A swimsuit; clothing worn for swimming.

How to Use It: On a hot summer day, Sophie called out, "Don't forget your bathers, we're heading to the beach." The word "bathers" is most common in southern states like Victoria and South Australia, while "swimmers" or "togs" are used elsewhere. It's a great example of regional Aussie slang.

Tip: Regional variation — "bathers" isn't used everywhere in Australia.

Beak

Definition: A slang term for someone's nose, especially a large or intrusive one.

How to Use It: When Sarah's uncle kept interrupting her conversation, she joked, "Keep your beak out of it, will ya?" The word "beak" works both literally, to describe a nose, and figuratively, for someone interfering where they shouldn't.

Beast

Definition: A huge, often old or battered car that's still impressive for its size.

How to Use It: When Mark pulled up in his rusted but oversized ute, his friend laughed, "You're still driving that beast?" Despite its dents and faded paint, the car was still running strong, hauling loads and handling rough tracks. The term is a compliment for a car that lasts.

Beaut

Definition: Short for "beauty," meaning great, excellent, or superb.

How to Use It: After finally fixing the barbecue, Mick grinned, "She's working again — beaut!" Aussies use the word to praise something done well, whether it's a good job, a lucky win, or a perfect day.

Berko

Definition: Slang for going berserk, acting wild, or losing control.

How to Use It: When the band hit the stage, the crowd went absolutely berko, jumping and shouting until the floor shook. The word is used to describe both good excitement and over-the-top behaviour. The tone decides if it's positive (fun) or negative (out of control).

Bevan

Definition: A derogatory term for someone considered silly, tacky, or a bit of a fool.

How to Use It: When Darren wore sunglasses at night to the pub, his mates laughed, "You look like a real bevan, mate." The word is often used to describe someone acting without class, dressing poorly, or showing off in a way that makes them look ridiculous. In Aussie culture, calling someone a "bevan" usually carries humour, but it can also sting if the person takes themselves too seriously.

Biffo

Definition: A scuffle, fight, or burst of rough play. Often used casually, not always seriously.

How to Use It: After the football match, two blokes started some friendly biffo in the car park, throwing light punches before laughing it off. The word "biffo" reflects Australia's casual approach to scraps, sometimes even seen as part of sporting culture or pub banter.

Tip: Informal. It can describe both harmless scuffles and genuine fights.

Bickie

Definition: Short for biscuit (cookie). It can also mean "money" in some contexts.

How to Use It: While having tea, Grandma said, "Grab a choccy bickie from the tin." In another context, you might hear, "That car costs a lot of bickies," where it refers to money. Aussies love their slang doing double duty, and "bickie" is a perfect example. This can also be spelled Bikkie.

Tip: Context is key — check if it means "snack" or "cash."

Big Smoke

Definition: A slang term for the city, particularly Sydney or Melbourne.

How to Use It: Heading into Sydney for a concert, Mel joked, "Off to the big smoke this weekend!" The phrase is often used by country folk to contrast their quieter lifestyle with the busy, crowded feel of Australia's largest cities.

Billy

Definition: Traditionally, a tin pot used to boil water over a campfire. More recently, it can also mean a bong for smoking.

How to Use It: Around the campfire, Tom said, "Let's put the billy on for some tea." In younger circles, though, "pass the billy" may mean something entirely different, referring to cannabis.

Tip: Generational split — older Aussies think "tea," younger ones may think "weed."

Billy Cart

Definition: A homemade go-kart, usually built from wood or scrap parts, often without an engine.

How to Use It: Kids in the suburbs raced their billy carts down the hill, steering wildly with ropes tied to the wheels. The phrase carries a sense of Aussie ingenuity — building fun out of whatever materials are on hand.

Big Whoop

Definition: A sarcastic way to downplay something that's being exaggerated.

How to Use It: When Liam bragged about eating ten hot dogs, his friend shrugged and said, "Big whoop." The phrase is used when someone tries to make a big deal out of something that isn't particularly impressive. It often carries a mocking or dismissive tone, cutting through the hype.

Birthday Suit

Definition: Slang for being completely naked.

How to Use It: After his shower, Dave forgot his towel and wandered through the hallway in his birthday suit, to the horror of his housemates. The phrase is light-hearted and often used in cheeky jokes about nudity.

Tip: Playful but can be inappropriate in formal settings.

Bite

Definition: To feel financial strain or pressure; also, it literally means to bite.

How to Use It: "The rent's really starting to bite this month," said Alex as he looked over the bills. In Aussie slang, the "bite" metaphor extends from physical pressure to the squeeze of money troubles.

Bitzer

Definition: A mixed-breed dog with no clear pedigree.

How to Use It: "What breed's your pup?" asked Sam. His friend laughed and said, "No idea, it's a bitzer." The word is often said with warmth, since many Aussies have fond memories of bitzers as tough, loyal, and no-fuss family pets. Unlike expensive purebred dogs, a bitzer is celebrated for being scrappy, adaptable, and uniquely Aussie.

Bizzo

Definition: Slang for business.

How to Use It: When asked why he was rushing, Max replied, "Got some bizzo to take care of." It's a relaxed way of saying "business," whether referring to actual work or personal matters.

Block

Definition: It can refer to a piece of land (often rural or agricultural) or someone's head.

How to Use It: "Bought a block out near Dubbo," Karen said proudly. In another context, her son muttered after a knock in footy, "Copped it right on the block." The word shifts meaning based on context, which is classic Aussie slang versatility.

Tip: Context is essential — it could mean property or simply "head."

Bloke

Definition: A man. The quintessential Australian term for a guy, often used affectionately.

How to Use It: "He's a good bloke," Emma said about her neighbour who helped fix her fence. The word captures the Aussie idea of the everyday, down-to-earth man — reliable, approachable, and easygoing. In Australian culture, being called a "top bloke" is one of the highest compliments. It suggests you're not just male, but you've got the honesty, generosity, and no-nonsense character that Aussies value.

Bloody

Definition: A classic Aussie intensifier, used to emphasise almost anything.

How to Use It: "That was a bloody great feed!" shouted Mick after a barbie. The word can express frustration, surprise, or enthusiasm, making it one of the most flexible Aussie fillers.

Tip: Common but still considered a mild swear word.

Bloody Oath

Definition: An emphatic "yes" or "absolutely."

How to Use It: When asked if he wanted to join the beach trip, Dave grinned and replied, "Bloody oath!" The phrase doesn't just mean yes — it carries weight, showing full-hearted agreement. Aussies use it to show enthusiasm, solidarity, or that something is unquestionably true. Whether at the pub, footy, or worksite, a "bloody oath" seals the deal with extra Aussie flair.

Bloody Galah

Definition: An insult for someone acting silly or obnoxious, comparing them to the noisy Australian bird.

How to Use It: When Rob tripped while clowning around, his friend laughed, "You bloody galah!" The phrase combines humour with mock annoyance, much like the screechy, disruptive bird it references. While often playful, it can also land as a genuine insult if used harshly.

Tip: Informal, light-hearted insult — not meant for strangers.

Blower

Definition: Slang for a breathalyser used by police to measure alcohol levels.

How to Use It: Pulled over after the footy, Ben was told by the officer, "Blow into the blower, mate." The term reflects the everyday Aussie tendency to shorten and nickname even serious tools.

Blow In

Definition: Someone who shows up unexpectedly, often without an invitation.

How to Use It: Midway through the barbecue, Tom grumbled, "Didn't expect Steve to blow in like that — hope we've got enough sausages." The term suggests someone arriving suddenly, almost as if carried by the wind.

Tip: It can sound rude if said directly to someone.

Blow Your Dough

Definition: To waste or spend all your money, often in one go.

How to Use It: "Went to the races and blew me dough on the first horse," Dave sighed. While it's often tied to gambling losses at the track or pokies, Aussies also use it for any reckless splurge — from dropping a week's pay at the pub to buying a flashy car you can't afford.

Bludge

Definition: To slack off, avoid work, or put in minimal effort.

How to Use It: "Stop bludging and give us a hand with the fence," yelled Mick to his friend lounging with a beer. The word is used at school, work, or anywhere someone's shirking responsibilities.

Bludger

Definition: A person who habitually avoids work or effort.

How to Use It: After spotting his housemate asleep again, John muttered, "You're a bloody bludger, mate." In Aussie slang, a bludger is someone who dodges responsibility — whether it's skipping shifts, leaving chores to others, or just slacking off while others pick up the slack. While it can be an insult, it's also often tossed around playfully in banter, especially when someone is caught taking it easy.

Tip: Common insult in Aussie English — but less harsh than it sounds.

Bomb

Definition: A car that's old, beat-up, and barely roadworthy.

How to Use It: "Still driving that bomb?" laughed Jenny as her friend's car backfired loudly. In Aussie slang, a "bomb" isn't just any old car — it's one that's noisy, dented, and sometimes held together with tape and luck. Despite looking like it belongs at the wreckers, a bomb is often treasured for its reliability or the memories tied to it. Many Aussies remember their first car being a bomb — the kind you drive to the pub, the footy, or just around town without worrying about scratches.

Boogie

Definition: To dance, or less commonly, to surf/swim (short for boogie board).

How to Use It: At the wedding reception, Jess grabbed her friend's hand and said, "Come on, let's have a boogie." The term usually means dancing, but in coastal towns, it may also mean catching waves.

Boogie Board

Definition: A short surfboard used for riding waves while lying down.

How to Use It: "The surf's too big for standing — I'll grab my boogie board instead," said Mick. The board is often used by beginners, but plenty of Aussies stick with it for fun at the beach.

Boomer

Definition: A large male kangaroo.

How to Use It: Pointing at the paddock, Sam exclaimed, "Look at that boomer — he's massive!" In Australia, a "boomer" refers specifically to a full-grown male kangaroo, known for their size, muscle, and dominance in the mob. Boomers can grow taller than a man and pack an intimidating punch (literally — kangaroos are famous for boxing). The word has long been part of bush life and folklore, well before the internet-era phrase "OK boomer" came along.

Boomerang

Definition: A traditional Aboriginal hunting tool designed to return when thrown.

How to Use It: At a cultural show, the guide demonstrated, "Throw it right and the boomerang comes straight back to you." The word is one of Australia's most globally recognised contributions to language and culture.

Booze Bus

Definition: A police bus set up to test drivers for alcohol levels.

How to Use It: "Slow down, mate, there's a booze bus up ahead," warned Jack as they drove past flashing lights. These mobile testing units are a common sight near events, pubs, or busy roads on weekends. The phrase is so common that most Aussies will instantly know it means a police alcohol checkpoint.

Boss Cocky

Definition: A farmer who employs others to work on their property.

How to Use It: Watching his neighbour order workers around, Dave chuckled, "He thinks he's boss cocky now." In Aussie slang, a "boss cocky" is more than just the farm owner — it's the one calling the shots, managing stockmen, shearers, or farmhands. The term reflects both authority and the no-nonsense leadership style often expected on rural properties.

Bottler

Definition: Something fantastic, impressive, or top quality.

How to Use It: After the gig, Emma grinned, "That band was a real bottler." The word can describe a performance, event, or even a person, showing strong approval in true Aussie style.

Bounce

Definition: A bully, often at school; someone who pushes others around.

How to Use It: "Don't be a bounce, leave him alone," snapped Karen when her friend teased another kid. While not as common today, the word still pops up in banter or older slang.

Brekkie

Definition: Breakfast.

How to Use It: "Let's grab some brekkie before work," suggested Sarah. The word is iconic Aussie slang, often used in cafés or casual chats. It reflects the Aussie habit of shortening words.

Brick Shithouse

Definition: Someone (usually a bloke) who is huge, strong, and solidly built.

How to Use It: Pointing at the footy player, Jake muttered, "He's built like a brick shithouse." The phrase is a classic Aussie way of describing a person with serious muscle and bulk — someone who looks immovable, like they've been carved out of concrete.

Tip: Crude and very informal.

Bright Spark

Definition: A clever or quick-witted person.

How to Use It: After solving a tricky problem, the teacher smiled, "You're a real bright spark." The phrase highlights someone who's sharp, switched on, or full of clever ideas. In Aussie English, it's often said with warmth, but depending on tone, it can also be used sarcastically — like when someone makes a silly mistake and a friend says, "Nice one, bright spark." Either way, it reflects the Aussie tendency to mix praise with humour, keeping things light-hearted.

Bring a Plate

Definition: To bring food to a party or gathering.

How to Use It: The barbecue invite read, "Just bring a plate and your own drinks." In Aussie culture, this means bring food to share, not an empty dish — a common mix-up for tourists.

Tip: Never turn up with just a plate — you'll look like a goose.

Brolly

Definition: Umbrella.

How to Use It: "Don't forget your brolly, looks like rain," said Mum before school. Like many Aussie shortenings, it adds a playful tone to an everyday item.

Bruce

Definition: A stereotypical Aussie bloke's name, often used to represent the everyday man.

How to Use It: "He's a real Bruce — hardworking, friendly, and always up for a yarn," said the neighbour. The name has become shorthand for the quintessential Aussie bloke.

Buck's Night

Definition: A bachelor party; a pre-wedding celebration for the groom and his friends.

How to Use It: "Got a buck's night this weekend — hope we survive it," laughed Dave. In Australia, a buck's night is rarely a quiet affair. It's usually packed with heavy drinking, cheeky pranks, and antics that the groom will never live down. Similar to the UK's "stag do," it's a rite of passage where mates send the groom off into married life with one last wild hurrah. Depending on the crowd, it can be a pub crawl, a big BBQ with endless slabs of beer, or an all-out weekend trip.

Buckley's Chance

Definition: Very little or no chance of success.

How to Use It: "You've got Buckley's chance of finishing that assignment tonight," joked Jess. The phrase comes from William Buckley, a convict who escaped in 1803 and lived with Aboriginal people — his survival seemed impossible, yet it became legend.

Bugalugs

Definition: A playful, often teasing nickname for someone, usually used in a friendly way.

How to Use It: When little Tommy walked into the room covered in jam, his grandma chuckled, "What are you up to, bugalugs?" The word is affectionate but not usually taken seriously.

Tip: Safe for kids, but adults might roll their eyes if you use it on them.

Bugger!

Definition: A mild exclamation, like "damn" or "oh no." It can be used in frustration or surprise.

How to Use It: Dropping his toast on the floor, Greg muttered, "Bugger!" Aussies love this word because it covers everything from small mistakes to big frustrations without being too offensive.

Tip: Considered mild enough to use around family — often taught to kids as their first "swear."

Bugger All

Definition: It means "nothing" or "very little."

How to Use It: "How much work did you get done today?" asked Sarah. Dan shrugged, "Bugger all." The phrase is casual shorthand for admitting you've achieved nothing or have very little of something.

Buggered

Definition: Extremely tired or exhausted. It can also mean broken or not working.

How to Use It: After moving house all day, Ben flopped onto the couch and groaned, "I'm buggered." In another sense, when his mate's old car wouldn't start, he added, "Looks like it's buggered too." The word is flexible — it can describe physical exhaustion, a busted object, or even a plan gone wrong.

Tip: Very common — from tradies to teenagers, everyone uses it.

Buggered If I Know

Definition: It means "I have no idea."

How to Use It: When asked where his keys were, Dave shrugged, "Buggered if I know, mate." The phrase is casual, direct, and carries a uniquely Aussie flavour of admitting cluelessness without embarrassment. It can be used for anything from small questions ("What's for dinner?") to bigger mysteries ("Why's the boss in a mood?"). The humour is in the delivery — it's both an answer and a way of brushing off worry.

Bugger Off!

Definition: It tells someone to go away; equivalent to "get lost."

How to Use It: When his brother kept pestering him for the TV remote, Josh snapped, "Bugger off!" Depending on tone, it can be playful banter or quite sharp.

Bull Bar

Definition: A strong metal bar fitted to the front of a vehicle to protect against animal collisions, especially kangaroos.

How to Use It: Pointing to the shiny new addition on his car, Steve said proudly, "Check out the bull bar — no roo's gonna smash this up." In rural Australia, a bull bar isn't just an accessory; it's a necessity. Kangaroos, wombats, and stray livestock often dart across country roads, and without a bull bar, a single hit can total a car. For many drivers, it's also a badge of pride, showing off a tough, bush-ready vehicle that can handle rough terrain and long drives.

Bum Bag

Definition: A small pouch or fanny pack worn around the waist.

How to Use It: At the music festival, Claire joked, "Check out my bum bag — hands free for dancing!" Once seen as daggy and only for tourists or dads on holiday, bum bags have made a full-blown fashion comeback. Today, you'll spot them slung across chests at music festivals, markets, or footy games. They're practical for carrying wallets, phones, and smokes, but they also carry a touch of Aussie irony — once laughed at, now worn with pride.

Tip: In the US, "fanny pack" is the term, but in Australia, never say "fanny" in public — it has a very different (and rude) meaning. Stick with "bum bag."

Bunch of Fives

Definition: A fist, especially one ready to throw a punch.

How to Use It: "Keep it up and you'll cop a bunch of fives," warned Mick, raising his hand. The phrase is old-school but still understood as a warning in arguments.

Bunyip

Definition: A creature from Aboriginal folklore said to lurk in swamps, rivers, and billabongs.

How to Use It: On a camping trip, kids whispered, "Don't go near the water at night, the bunyip will get ya!" The legend is part of Australia's mythology, blending Indigenous storytelling with modern spooky tales.

Burnout

Definition: Spinning a car's wheels so the tyres smoke, often done in car parks or paddocks for show.

How to Use It: After getting his license, Jack couldn't resist pulling a burnout in the Macca's (McDonald's) car park, tyres screeching as smoke filled the air. In Aussie culture, burnouts are seen as a mix of mischief and bragging rights.

Tip: Illegal on public roads — mostly linked with hoon culture.

Burl

Definition: A try or an attempt at something.

How to Use It: "Never bowled before, but I'll give it a burl," laughed Tom at the cricket nets. The phrase is friendly encouragement to have a go, no matter the outcome.

Bush

Definition: Refers to rural or remote areas outside cities and towns.

How to Use It: "I'm heading back to the bush this weekend," Sarah told her workmates, meaning a trip to her hometown, hours away from the city. In Australia, "the bush" symbolises rugged living, nature, and life away from urban centres.

Bush Week

Definition: A made-up event, used sarcastically to mock someone for acting naïve or unsophisticated.

How to Use It: When Tom walked into the city barefoot, his friend laughed, "What is this, bush week?" The phrase pokes fun at out-of-place behaviour that looks rough or outback-style.

Tip: It can come across as condescending if aimed at strangers.

Bushranger

Definition: Outlaws of the nineteenth century who roamed the Australian bush, often robbing travellers and coaches.

How to Use It: Touring rural Victoria, the guide explained, "Ned Kelly was the most famous bushranger — half villain, half folk hero." The word carries historical weight, tied to Australia's colonial past and legends of rebellion.

Bust

Definition: To be caught by police or to go broke.

How to Use It: After the cops pulled up outside the shed, Jake whispered, "Reckon we're about to get busted." The word "bust" is common in crime and money talk, meaning either being arrested or going financially under.

Tip: Very casual and linked with trouble — avoid in formal settings.

By Jingoes

Definition: An old-fashioned exclamation of surprise or amazement.

How to Use It: Watching his horse win against the odds, the old-timer cheered, "By jingoes, what a finish!" The phrase has a distinctly old-school charm and is now used more playfully or in a nostalgic sense. It's rarely used seriously today.

BYO

Definition: Bring Your Own — usually alcohol, sometimes food.

How to Use It: The party invite read, "BBQ at mine, BYO drinks." The phrase is a staple of Aussie gatherings, from backyard barbies to restaurants that don't serve alcohol.

Tip: Common on signs and invitations — safe to use everywhere.

C

Cackhanded

Definition: Clumsy, awkward, or lacking coordination.

How to Use It: Struggling to roll a swag, Pete laughed at himself, "I'm so cackhanded with this thing." The phrase highlights both physical clumsiness and social awkwardness, making it versatile. It's used playfully between mates, but calling someone "cackhanded" can sting if said harshly.

Cakehole

Definition: A slang word for mouth. Usually used when telling someone to be quiet.

How to Use It: During a heated game of pool, Mick snapped, "Shut your cakehole and take the shot." Though cheeky, it reflects the Aussie love of colourful insults.

Tip: It sounds aggressive, but among mates it's more playful than hostile.

Canary

Definition: A defect notice slapped on a car by police, marking it unroadworthy.

How to Use It: Pointing to the bright yellow sticker, Dave groaned, "Got a bloody canary on me car." The term is everyday Aussie motoring slang, dreaded by drivers across the country.

Tip: A "canary" doesn't mean your car is done for — it just needs fixing before you can drive it legally again.

Cane Toad

Definition: A Queenslander. Also refers to the actual cane toads — toxic pests introduced to Australia in the 1930s.

How to Use It: At State of Origin, a NSW fan yelled, "Go home, you bloody cane toads!" The term blends regional rivalry with the infamous pest, making it both playful and cutting.

Tip: Harmless between sports fans, but don't throw it at a stranger outside the footy — it may not land well.

Camp Oven

Definition: A heavy cast-iron pot used on campfires to cook meals outdoors.

How to Use It: Around the fire, Jack said, "Chucked a lamb roast in the camp oven — give it an hour." The camp oven isn't just cookware, it's part of bush culture — a way to cook everything from damper to stew when camping.

Caper

Definition: A person's line of work or area of activity; sometimes used for "scheme" or "job."

How to Use It: When asked what he does, Mark shrugged, "Writing's my caper, keeps me busy." The phrase often sounds more laid-back than saying "career" — a reminder that Aussies prefer keeping things casual, even when talking about work.

Carpet Grubs

Definition: Slang for babies or toddlers crawling on the floor.

How to Use It: At the family BBQ, Aunt June laughed, "Keep the carpet grubs away from the esky." The term is cheeky and affectionate, poking fun at little kids who get into everything.

Tip: Often used jokingly among family and friends — not meant as an insult.

Cark It

Definition: To die, or for something to break down.

How to Use It: "Thought my car was about to cark it on the highway," joked Mick. The phrase is blunt but widely used, whether for machines or people. While dark, Aussies use it casually, reflecting the national tendency to joke about serious things.

Tip: Normal between mates, but avoid using it lightly if someone's actually grieving.

Catch Forty Winks

Definition: To take a nap or short sleep.

How to Use It: "I'll catch forty winks before the night shift," said John, stretching out on the couch. Aussies use it to talk about sneaky naps — from tradies in their cars to office workers ducking off for a lunchtime snooze.

Centralia

Definition: The middle of Australia — essentially, the desert heart where there's not much around.

How to Use It: "Driving through Centralia is a long haul — nothing but red dirt for hours," said Karen. The word reflects both geography and Aussie humour about the sheer emptiness of the Outback.

Chalkie

Definition: A schoolteacher, named for their old reliance on blackboards and chalk.

How to Use It: "Old Mr. Thompson was my chalkie back in Year 6," laughed Dave. The nickname highlights Aussie culture's habit of shortening words and making jobs sound more casual — even when referring to authority figures like teachers.

Champers

Definition: Champagne, usually used in casual or celebratory contexts.

How to Use It: At New Year's, Sarah raised her glass and said, "Nothing like a bit of champers to kick things off." Aussies use it to keep fancy drinks sounding down-to-earth. Even though champagne is often tied to luxury, "champers" makes it feel more approachable and fun.

Cheers

Definition: More than just a drinking toast, in Australia *cheers* is everyday shorthand for "thanks." It's casual, friendly, and works just as well when someone hands you a beer as when they send you an email.

How to Use It: "Cheers for the lift, mate," said Tom as he hopped out of the ute.

Tip: Aussies use it so often that it can replace "thank you" almost anywhere — just keep it light and informal.

Cheerio

Definition: A cheeky or sarcastic way to say goodbye.

How to Use It: After pranking his friend by hiding the car keys, Tom waved and said, "Cheerio, see you at the pub!" The word adds humour to a farewell, making it sound old-fashioned but still cheeky.

Chew and Spew

Definition: Slang for a low-quality fast-food joint.

How to Use It: "Let's skip that chew and spew — last time it made me crook," said Anna. The phrase captures the Aussie way of using blunt, funny imagery to describe something everyone recognises.

Chewie

Definition: Chewing gum.

How to Use It: "Got a spare chewie?" asked Lisa before her meeting. Shortened words like this are classic Aussie slang — practical, quick, and often used by younger people.

Chinwag

Definition: A casual chat, often gossip or small talk.

How to Use It: "Stopped for a chinwag with the neighbour over the fence," said Sharon. It captures the Aussie love of informal conversation — the kind that can stretch for ages about footy, weather, or local news.

Choc-a-bloc

Definition: Completely full, crowded, or overflowing.

How to Use It: "The train was choc-a-bloc this morning," groaned Megan as she squeezed into the carriage. The phrase paints a vivid picture of being packed to the brim — whether it's a fridge stuffed with leftovers, a pub heaving on Friday night, or a beach crammed on Christmas Day. Aussies use it for anything overloaded, not just places with people.

Choof Off

Definition: To leave or go away. Also linked to slang for marijuana.

How to Use It: "Better choof off before the rain hits," said Tom as he packed up the ute. In one sense, it's just a casual way to say "head off" or "move along." But in another, mates might use it when talking about lighting up a joint, so the meaning depends heavily on context. Aussies often love the double-entendre, so you'll hear it in both everyday farewells and cheeky conversations.

Chop and Change

Definition: To keep switching decisions, plans, or approaches.

How to Use It: "She keeps chopping and changing about the holiday plans," sighed Paul. The phrase is often used in frustration, highlighting indecisiveness.

Choppers

Definition: Teeth, often false ones.

How to Use It: "Grandad lost his choppers again," laughed Jack. While it can simply mean teeth, it's often used jokingly, especially when talking about dentures.

Chuck a Sickie

Definition: To call in sick at work — often faked — usually to have a day off for leisure.

How to Use It: "Too good a day to be stuck in the office — I'll chuck a sickie," laughed Rob as he packed his esky for the beach. The phrase is more than just skipping work — it's part of Aussie workplace culture. A "sickie" might be genuine, but when someone says they're "chucking one," it usually means they're having a sneaky day off for sport, or simply a kip.

Chrissie

Definition: Christmas.

How to Use It: "Heading to the coast for Chrissie," said Amy. Like many Aussie shortenings, it makes the holiday sound relaxed and casual — more about family, beach, and barbies than formality.

Chuck a U-ie

Definition: To make a U-turn while driving.

How to Use It: "Missed the exit, gotta chuck a U-ie," sighed Steve. The phrase reflects how Aussies simplify and shorten even the most ordinary tasks.

Ciggy

Definition: A cigarette.

How to Use It: "Step outside for a ciggy?" asked Mark during smoko. Short, casual, and widely used, it's one of the most common slang terms across all groups.

Clod-Hoppers

Definition: Oversized or clumsy shoes that look awkward or out of place.

How to Use It: "What are those clod-hoppers on your feet? You off to the circus?" teased Mark. Aussies use it when someone's footwear looks comically large or impractical. It's more playful than nasty, often said in light-hearted ribbing.

Tip: Best used in banter — not as an actual fashion critique!

Clucky

Definition: It describes a woman (or occasionally a man) feeling maternal and wanting kids.

How to Use It: After holding her friend's baby, Jess sighed, "I'm feeling a bit clucky." The term is everyday Aussie shorthand for that "baby fever" moment. It can also be used jokingly if someone fusses over pets, kids, or even plants.

Tip: Light-hearted — but be cautious, since it touches on personal feelings.

Cobber

Definition: An old-fashioned but affectionate word for "mate" or close friend.

How to Use It: "Thanks for the help, cobber," said Tom as his mate lifted the heavy box. While less common today, it still pops up in rural areas and among older generations. Using it adds a warm, nostalgic flavour to Aussie banter.

Cockie

Definition: Short for cockatoo — noisy, cheeky, and often destructive birds found all over Australia. By extension, it can also describe someone who's cocky: overconfident, cheeky, or a bit arrogant.

How to Use It: "Bloody cockies stripped the fruit trees again," groaned Dave, watching the flock squawk overhead. At the same time, when Sam bragged about winning every hand of cards, his mate teased, "Don't be so cockie, mate." The word works both ways — either for the bold, noisy birds Aussies complain about (and secretly adore) or for people acting just as loud and overconfident.

Cockroach

Definition: Slang for someone from New South Wales, especially in the State of Origin rugby rivalry.

How to Use It: "We're up against the cockroaches tonight," said a Queensland fan. The nickname is mocking but tied to sporting banter, much like "Cane Toad" for Queenslanders.

Tip: Mostly for rugby contexts — using it outside sport can sound odd.

Cock-Up

Definition: A mess-up or big mistake.

How to Use It: "Well, that's a cock-up if I've ever seen one," muttered John after spilling beer over the BBQ. Aussies use it for anything from small blunders to major disasters, often with humour to soften the sting.

Come to Blows

Definition: When an argument escalates into a physical fight.

How to Use It: "Those two nearly came to blows over the footy score," said Mark. While serious, the phrase is often used in storytelling, turning fights into pub anecdotes.

Compo

Definition: Short for compensation, often financial.

How to Use It: "He's on compo after that accident at work," explained Sue over a pint. In Aussie slang, "compo" is a common pub topic — whether someone's mate scored a payout after slipping on the job, or a tradie is off work with an injury but still getting paid. It's often said with a mix of sympathy and envy, as compo can mean a break from work with money still rolling in.

Cooking with Gas

Definition: To be making great progress or doing something effectively.

How to Use It: After hours of struggling with the BBQ, Pete finally got it going and grinned, "Now we're cooking with gas!" Aussies use it whenever things finally click into place.

Note: The phrase came from old gas stove ads but stuck around as a way to celebrate momentum.

Cop It Sweet

Definition: To accept punishment, criticism, or a tough situation without complaint.

How to Use It: When fined for speeding, Jack shrugged, "Fair enough, I'll cop it sweet." It shows resilience and an Aussie tendency to face consequences head-on — or at least without whingeing.

Coppers

Definition: Slang for the police.

How to Use It: "Better hide the beers, the coppers are coming," whispered Mick at a beach party. It's often used with cheeky disrespect but also everyday familiarity.

Tip: Widely understood, but very casual — best kept to jokes or stories.

Corroboree

Definition: A traditional Aboriginal gathering with dance, music, and ceremony. Sometimes also used for informal Indigenous community gatherings.

How to Use It: "We were invited to a corroboree by the local mob," said Sarah. The word has cultural weight and should be used respectfully when referring to Aboriginal traditions.

Tip: Unlike most slang here, this is deeply tied to First Nations culture — avoid casual misuse.

Crack Onto

Definition: To flirt with or try to pick someone up.

How to Use It: That bloke's trying to crack onto you at the bar," whispered Jane as her friend rolled her eyes. In Aussie slang, "crack onto" is used when someone is making their interest clear — whether it's smooth chatting or clumsy, tipsy flirting after a few cold ones. It can be playful, cheeky, or downright unwanted, depending on the situation.

Crapper

Definition: Slang for the toilet.

How to Use It: "Where's the crapper?" asked Baz at the pub. It's casual, blunt, and still widely recognised, though "dunny" is more iconic Aussie slang.

Creepy-Crawley

Definition: Insects, bugs, or anything small and unsettling that crawls.

How to Use It: "Check for creepy-crawlies before you hop in the swag," warned Mick. The word is often used with kids, but adults use it just as often when confronted with Aussie-sized spiders.

Crash Hot

Definition: Very impressive — though often used in the negative ("not crash hot").

How to Use It: "That pie wasn't crash hot," muttered Dan after a servo stop. The phrase fits Aussie understatement, where even praise is usually delivered modestly.

Crook

Definition: Sick, unwell, or dodgy. It can also mean angry ("go crook").

How to Use It: "Can't come to work, feeling crook," texted Jess. In another sense: "He went crook at me for being late." The double meaning makes it versatile Aussie slang.

Crow Eater

Definition: A person from South Australia.

How to Use It: "Typical crow eater bragging about wine again," teased a Victorian. It's used mostly in sporting or state rivalry banter, tied to the stereotype of South Australians once eating crows in hard times.

Crikey

Definition: A classic Aussie exclamation of surprise or shock, similar to saying "wow" or "oh my gosh." It can express amazement, disbelief, or even mild frustration. Made famous worldwide by Steve Irwin, the Crocodile Hunter.

How to Use It: "Crikey, that roo nearly jumped in front of the ute!" gasped Mick, gripping the wheel.

Tip: It's old-school Aussie, but still loved for its charm. Use it when you want your reaction to sound authentically down under.

Cubby House

Definition: A small playhouse for kids, usually built in the backyard.

How to Use It: "The kids are in the cubby house pretending it's a castle," said Sarah. Many Aussies have childhood memories of cubby houses, from makeshift sheet forts to fancy timber builds.

Tip: A nostalgic, family-friendly word that brings out Aussie backyard culture.

Cuppa

Definition: A cup of tea or coffee.

How to Use It: "Come in for a cuppa, love," said Nan. The phrase reflects Aussie hospitality — tea or coffee is less about the drink itself and more about taking time to chat.

Note: Simple, warm, and one of the most enduring Aussie-isms.

Cut Lunch

Definition: A packed lunch brought from home, often sandwiches.

How to Use It: "Mum gave me a cut lunch — ham sangas again," sighed Tim at school. For tradies and kids alike, it's the classic way to describe a simple homemade feed. The term connotes strong Aussie schoolyard and worksite nostalgia.

Cut Up

Definition: To be upset, criticised, or deeply affected.

How to Use It: "He was pretty cut up after losing his dog," said Lisa softly. In another sense: "She was cut up in the meeting for missing the deadline." It can describe both emotional hurt and harsh criticism.

Tip: Context tells you if it's about feelings or being put down.

D

Dacks

Definition: Aussie slang for pants, often loose-fitting tracksuit pants or casual trousers.

How to Use It: "Forgot me dacks at the gym, had to drive home in me footy shorts," laughed Baz. The word is a staple of everyday slang, often tied to comfort and homewear. Some playful variations include *tracky dacks* for tracksuit pants and *reg grundies* (rhyming slang) for undies.

Dag

Definition: Someone uncool, socially awkward, or out of touch with trends — but often in an endearing way.

How to Use It: "He's a bit of a dag, still tucks his shirt into his jeans," joked Sarah. Unlike harsher insults, "dag" can carry affection, especially when describing quirky, lovable people who don't follow fashion.

Damage

Definition: Slang for the amount of alcohol consumed, or more broadly, the toll taken by a big night.

How to Use It: "What's the damage from last night?" asked Liam, counting empty stubbies on the table. It can also be used in pubs to ask for the bill, tying directly to Aussie drinking culture.

Tip: Still widely used today, especially in reference to bar tabs or heavy drinking sessions.

Damper

Definition: A traditional bush bread made from flour, water, and sometimes milk, baked over campfires.

How to Use It: "We made fresh damper in the camp oven last night," said Jack, tearing into the crusty loaf. Damper is iconic in Aussie bush cooking, often eaten with golden syrup or butter. It represents self-sufficiency and the bush lifestyle. It's still popular on camping trips, even though most Aussies buy their bread from the supermarket today.

Darwin Stubbie

Definition: A giant beer bottle holding 2.25 litres (or seventy-six ounces), unique to Australia's Northern Territory.

How to Use It: "Picked up a Darwin stubbie for the weekend — that'll do me," laughed Harry, showing off the massive bottle. More than just a drink, the Darwin stubbie is a quirky icon of Aussie pub culture. It first appeared in the 1950s and quickly became tied to the NT's reputation for going big — big distances, big crocs, and big beers.

Dead Marine

Definition: An empty beer bottle.

How to Use It: "Clear up the dead marines before the next round," ordered Mick. The phrase adds a touch of humour, likening spent bottles to fallen soldiers after a heavy session.

Deadset

Definition: Used to stress truth, sincerity, or surprise. It can mean "seriously" or "for real."

How to Use It: "Deadset, that was the best game I've seen all season," said Karen, shaking her head in disbelief. The word works in many tones — it can show shock ("Deadset? You're moving to Perth?"), agreement ("That's deadset true, mate"), or even frustration ("This traffic is deadset ridiculous").

Its versatility makes it one of the most distinctly Aussie terms — short, punchy, and perfect for cutting straight to the point.

Defo

Definition: Short for "definitely."

How to Use It: "Coming to the footy this weekend?" asked Sam. His brother replied, "Defo, mate — wouldn't miss it." The word shows the Aussie tendency to shorten even the most common expressions, keeping conversations fast and casual.

Dekko

Definition: Slang for "a look" or "a glance." It comes from Hindi, brought into Aussie English through British colonial ties.

How to Use It: "Have a dekko at this old photo album," said June, handing it around at the family BBQ. The word feels playful and has a touch of old-school charm, often used by older generations.

Tip: Not as common among younger Aussies today but still well understood.

Deli

Definition: Short for delicatessen. In Australia, it can mean either a small corner store or a shop selling cold meats and cheeses, depending on the region.

How to Use It: "Gonna grab some ham and cheese from the deli for sangas," said Tom. For many Aussies, the local deli is part of daily life, whether it's for snacks, cigarettes, or lunch meat. In South Australia, "deli" often means a corner shop — elsewhere, it usually means a specialty store.

Der

Definition: The Aussie version of "duh," used to mock someone for saying something obvious.

How to Use It: "Water's wet," said Jack. His sister rolled her eyes and replied, "Yeah, der." The word is short, sharp, and carries that sarcastic edge perfect for sibling banter or friends ribbing each other.

Dero

Definition: Short for "derelict." It refers to someone down-and-out, often associated with rough sleeping or heavy drinking, but it can also be used jokingly among mates.

How to Use It: "You slept in the garden after the party? You're such a dero," laughed Tom. It can be harsh when aimed at strangers, but between friends, it's more cheeky than cruel.

Devo

Definition: Short for "devastated," meaning very upset or disappointed.

How to Use It: "The pub ran out of VB? I'm devo," groaned Baz. The word keeps even serious disappointment sounding casual, which is very Aussie — making bad news feel lighter with humour.

Dim Sims

Definition: A dumpling-like Chinese snack adapted to Australian tastes, often deep-fried and sold at fish and chip shops.

How to Use It: "Grab us some fish, chips, and a couple of dimmies," said Steve at the takeaway counter. Unlike traditional Chinese dumplings, dim sims are uniquely Aussie and have become a nostalgic comfort food for many. They are also usually called "dimmies" in casual speech.

Ding

Definition: Minor damage to a vehicle, usually from a bump or collision.

How to Use It: "Backed into a post and put a ding in me ute," sighed Mick. The word is casual, used when damage is annoying but not catastrophic — part of the everyday hazards of Aussie driving.

Dingbat

Definition: A fool, idiot, or someone acting silly.

How to Use It: "Only a dingbat would try to surf in a storm," muttered Jess, watching her friend get wiped out by a massive wave. The word covers a wide range — from someone making a harmless mistake (like forgetting their sunnies on a forty-degree day) to someone doing something downright reckless. Depending on tone, it can be a sharp insult or a playful dig among friends. Its flexibility keeps it alive in both everyday chat and light-hearted ribbing.

Dink

Definition: To give someone a ride on the back or front of a bicycle or motorbike.

How to Use It: "Hop on, I'll dink ya to the servo," said Kyle, patting the handlebars. For many Aussies, being dinked as a kid — wobbling dangerously while holding tight — is a rite of passage.

Dinky-Di

Definition: True, genuine, or the real deal.

How to Use It: "That pie shop's dinky-di Aussie," said Baz, biting into a hot meat pie. The phrase adds emphasis, showing something is authentically Australian or honest. It's often used with pride when praising traditions, food, or people.

Dipstick

Definition: A silly, foolish, or clueless person.

How to Use It: "You left the esky open, ya dipstick — now the ice is gone," groaned Mark. Aussies use it when mates make dumb mistakes. It's usually playful, but depending on tone, it can sting.

Tip: A classic insult in banter — not deeply offensive, but don't toss it at strangers.

Doona

Definition: A quilt or duvet used for sleeping.

How to Use It: "Too cold to get out from under the doona this morning," said Anna. In Aussie winters, doonas are practically sacred, and the word itself feels cosy — tied to comfort, warmth, and lazy mornings.

Dole

Definition: Welfare payments given by Centrelink or other government services.

How to Use It: "Been on the dole a few months since I lost me job," admitted Kev. For many Aussies, the word carries both humour and stigma — it can mean survival support or lazy bludging, depending on who's saying it.

Tip: Sensitive term — can offend if used carelessly.

Dropkick

Definition: Someone considered useless, foolish, or hopeless.

How to Use It: "Only a dropkick would forget the snags for a barbie," joked Phil. It's often said in banter among mates, but it can cut deeper if used seriously.

Tip: Insulting if taken literally — keep it light-hearted.

Drongo

Definition: A fool, idiot, or someone who lacks common sense.

How to Use It: "Forgot his wallet at the servo again — what a drongo," sighed Mark. Originally the name of a racehorse that never won, the word stuck as Aussie slang for someone hopeless or slow.

Drum

Definition: Slang for information, a tip-off, or sometimes a container/barrel.

How to Use It: "What's the drum on the new pub opening?" asked Mick, eager to hear the latest goss. In Aussie slang, "drum" often means inside knowledge or a reliable heads-up, especially about local news, bargains, or sporting events. It can also literally mean a barrel or container, but in conversation it nearly always leans towards "the info."

Dubbo

Definition: A country town in New South Wales. Sometimes also used (cheekily) to imply someone's a bit simple.

How to Use It: "She's moving out to Dubbo for work," said Kate. The place name is neutral, but in banter, "ya dubbo" can mean a bit of a dope.

Tip: Be careful — context decides if it's affectionate or insulting.

Duff

Definition: Pregnant — often used in the sense of an unplanned or surprising pregnancy.

How to Use It: "Turns out Stacey's up the duff," whispered Karen at the BBQ. Aussies use "duff" in casual gossip or light-hearted chatter, especially when a pregnancy wasn't exactly planned. It carries a cheeky, informal tone.

Duffer

Definition: Someone considered clumsy, foolish, or a bit of an idiot. Historically, it also referred to cattle thieves who rebranded stolen livestock.

How to Use It: "Forgot his lunch again? You're a real duffer," laughed Sarah at her friend. The word can be affectionate ribbing for small mistakes, but its bushranger history gives it an extra Aussie flavour.

Dust-Up

Definition: A fight, brawl, or heated argument.

How to Use It: "There was a dust-up outside the footy club after the game," reported Ben. It captures the image of fists flying and dirt being kicked up, though it can also mean a loud verbal clash.

E

Earbash

Definition: To talk endlessly, often in a way that's annoying or unhelpful.

How to Use It: "Don't earbash me about your diet, I just want a beer," groaned Mick. To "earbash" someone is to hammer them with chatter until they're worn out. It's often used when the talk is repetitive, dull, or one-sided.

Ears Flapping

Definition: Someone who is listening intently, often to gossip.

How to Use It: "The kids were supposed to be asleep, but I saw their ears flapping behind the couch," laughed Jane. The phrase suggests someone quietly soaking up every word, whether they're meant to be listening or not.

Easy As

Definition: Shortened version of "easy as pie" — meaning simple or no trouble at all.

How to Use It: "Installing the new app? Easy as, mate," said Josh. Aussies love trimming phrases down, and "easy as" gets the job done fast. It often comes with an unspoken comparison — easy as pie, cake, or whatever you fancy.

Eat a Horse

Definition: To be extremely hungry.

How to Use It: "Haven't eaten all day, I could eat a horse," said Dan as he opened the fridge. The phrase exaggerates hunger, a classic Aussie way of making a point. It's heard everywhere from family kitchens to pubs after a long day's work.

Elbow Grease

Definition: Hard physical effort, especially in cleaning or manual work.

How to Use It: "The ute's filthy — bit of elbow grease and she'll shine again," said Baz. The phrase is used when the job requires muscle and persistence, not shortcuts. It's a favourite among tradies, bosses, and parents giving kids chores.

El Cheapo

Definition: Something inexpensive, often of poor quality.

How to Use It: "Couldn't afford the good stuff, so I grabbed an el cheapo bottle of wine," laughed Dave. The phrase often carries a mix of humour and honesty — Aussies are quick to admit when they've gone for the budget option.

Esky

Definition: A portable cooler for keeping drinks and food cold. Originally a brand name, now used generically.

How to Use It: "Throw the snags and beers in the esky, we're off to the beach," said Tom. In Australia, no picnic, camping trip, or footy game is complete without one. It's a symbol of summer, friendship, and keeping coldies icy.

Even Steven

Definition: To be equal or on fair terms with someone.

How to Use It: After losing a bet but then winning a round of pool, Jack grinned, "Guess we're even steven now, mate." The phrase reflects the Aussie sense of fairness — balancing the score so no one's left owing.

Exy

Definition: Short for "expensive."

How to Use It: "Nah, mate, those concert tickets are way too exy," groaned Baz. Aussies love shortening words, and "exy" is the quick, casual way to complain about cost — whether it's housing, beer, or avocados.

F

Face Ache

Definition: Not an actual ache, but a miserable or sour-looking face.

How to Use It: "Deadset boss, ya gotta do something about ya face ache," said Baz. The term is often used in cheeky banter to lighten the mood, even if someone really is upset. In Aussie culture, it reflects the tendency to call out negativity in a playful way rather than let it linger.

Tip: It works best in friendly settings — not when someone's genuinely grieving.

Fag

Definition: Slang for a cigarette, borrowed from Britain.

How to Use It: "Pass us a fag, would ya?" said Pete on smoko. While still common in Australia, it's mostly used by older generations. Younger Aussies are more likely to say *ciggy*.

Tip: Be careful outside Australia and the UK — in other countries, it can be offensive.

Fair Dinkum

Definition: Genuinely true, sincere, or authentic.

How to Use It: "That bloke's got a fair dinkum talent for footy," said the coach. The phrase has become one of the most iconic Aussie expressions, used to confirm honesty, express admiration, or stress seriousness.

Tip: It can also be a question — "Fair dinkum?" = "Really?"

Fair Enough

Definition: Expression of acceptance, agreement, or understanding.

How to Use It: "I hate footy," said James. "Fair enough, mate," replied Chris. Aussies use it as a polite way to end disagreements without creating tension. It's one of those easygoing phrases that keeps conversations smooth.

Fair Go, Mate!

Definition: A call for fairness, usually when someone feels hard done by.

How to Use It: "Oi, fair go, mate! I was here first," yelled John when someone jumped the servo queue. It carries a mix of frustration and Aussie insistence on being treated fairly. It's often used in arguments, but also jokingly when mates muck around.

Fairy Bread

Definition: A kids' party snack — white bread with butter and sprinkles.

How to Use It: "No fairy bread at the party? That's un-Australian," laughed Lisa. It's nostalgic comfort food, tied to childhood memories, but often makes cheeky appearances at adult parties too.

Tip: Instantly sparks Aussie nostalgia.

Fang It

Definition: To go full speed or push hard at something, usually driving.

How to Use It: "Fang it down the highway, we're late for kick-off!" yelled Harry. While most often tied to hooning cars or revving a ute, Aussies also stretch it to sport and effort — "fang it at training" or "fang it at work" means going all out. The word carries energy, cheek, and recklessness, which is why it's used with both admiration and mockery.

Tip: Playful but also tied to reckless driving — so better for jokes than advice!

Fanny

Definition: In Australia, it means vagina. (Different from the UK, where it means bum.)

How to Use It: "He said fanny in front of the Poms — they nearly choked laughing," said Sarah. This word is one of the great cultural mix-ups: an Aussie says it means female genitals, while a Brit hears it as backside. The double meaning makes it both a slang trap for travellers and a cheeky source of humour. In Aussie use, it's crude, often dropped in blokey banter or as a schoolyard giggle-word.

Fart-Arsing

Definition: Wasting time or being silly instead of doing something useful.

How to Use It: "Stop fart-arsing around and finish the job," snapped the foreman. It's used in frustration but can also be used jokingly when friends are messing about.

Tip: Common in workplaces, especially tradie banter.

Feel Crook

Definition: To feel unwell or sick.

How to Use It: "Can't come to work today, feel crook as," texted Sharon. It's everyday slang for sickness, whether it's a cold, a hangover, or food poisoning. "Crook" can also describe something broken ("the telly's crook").

Figjam

Definition: Acronym for "F*ck I'm Good, Just Ask Me" — someone arrogant or full of themselves.

How to Use It: "He strutted in like a real figjam, talking up his golf swing," muttered Baz. The term captures Aussie dislike for people who brag too much.

Tip: Usually said behind someone's back, not to their face.

Filthy

Definition: Very angry or upset.

How to Use It: "Missed the grand final tickets — I'm filthy," groaned Dan. Aussies often use *filthy* to express strong emotion, but the beauty is in its range. It can be pure rage ("I'm filthy with the ref's call") or everyday frustration ("The shop's out of pies, I'm filthy"). In banter, it softens what could otherwise sound aggressive, turning anger into humour."

Tip: Tone matters — in friendly banter, it sounds lighter than "furious."

Fire Away

Definition: An invitation to speak, ask questions, or share ideas.

How to Use It: "Got a question about the job? Fire away," said the boss. Aussies love straightforwardness, and this phrase is a friendly green light that encourages open talk. While you'll hear it in workplaces, teachers' rooms, or interviews, friends also use it in casual settings — "Fire away with the next story, Harry." The phrase mixes informality with encouragement, making it versatile across settings.

Fisho

Definition: A fishmonger or seafood shop.

How to Use It: "Swing by the fisho for some prawns," said Mum. It's shorthand for a place — or the bloke — selling seafood.

Tip: Common in coastal towns where seafood is a daily staple.

Five-Finger Discount

Definition: Slang for stealing (shoplifting).

How to Use It: "Nicked a choccy bar with the ol' five-finger discount," bragged Damo. The phrase carries humour, though it refers to theft.

Tip: Said jokingly — not wise to admit seriously!

Flake

Definition: Fried fillet of gummy shark, sold at Aussie fish and chip shops.

How to Use It: "Grab us some chips and a piece of flake," said Mick at the takeaway. It's a staple of Aussie fast-food culture, especially in Victoria. Many tourists don't realise "flake" means shark meat — locals do.

Fleabag

Definition: Something dirty, messy, or someone unkempt.

How to Use It: "That pub's a bit of a fleabag, but the beer's cheap," shrugged Paul. While it's often applied to run-down places — old hotels, dodgy bars, messy cars — it can also be aimed at people, usually with humour. Calling someone a fleabag suggests they're in need of a wash or tidy-up, but still in a fond, ribbing tone.

Flick

Definition: To get rid of something or someone, or a photo.

How to Use It: "Got the flick from work," said Baz. Here, it means sacked. In another sense: "Send us that party flick," where it means photo. It also appears in relationships ("She gave him the flick") or objects ("Flicked the old ute for a new one"). The dual meaning makes it a classic Aussie shorthand — practical, casual, and cheeky.

Footy

Definition: Short for Australian Rules Football (AFL) or sometimes rugby league, depending on the state.

How to Use It: "Watching the footy this arvo?" asked Ben. In Victoria and SA, it means AFL; in NSW and QLD, it's usually rugby league. Either way, footy is almost a religion.

Freshie

Definition: A freshwater crocodile, smaller and less dangerous than the saltie.

How to Use It: "Saw a freshie up near Katherine Gorge," said Tim. While they're not as feared as salties, Aussies still talk about freshies with caution — a reminder that even "less scary" crocs can bite.

Frothing

Definition: Extremely excited or eager.

How to Use It: "I'm frothing for the game tonight," grinned Dan. The term captures bubbling-over enthusiasm, like the head of a beer. Aussies use it for footy, music gigs, or even just heading to the pub — it's more intense than "keen."

Fuck All

Definition: Nothing, or very little.

How to Use It: "Did fuck all at work today," admitted Sam. The phrase is blunt and versatile, used for tasks, money, effort, or results. Despite being coarse, it's so common that most Aussies hardly notice the swearing.

Tip: Definitely informal — keep it for friends, not your boss.

G

G'day

Definition: A cheerful Aussie greeting, short for "good day."

How to Use It: "G'day, how's it going?" is about as Australian as it gets. It works with strangers, friends, or even at work. It's simple, warm, and instantly identifies you as an Aussie (or someone trying to sound like one).

Tip: It can be used any time of day — morning, noon, or night.

Gab

Definition: To chat, often gossip or silly talk.

How to Use It: "Let's grab a pint and have a gab," said Kelly. A gab can be deep and meaningful, but more often it's about who's dating whom or what drama is unfolding. Aussies love a gab in beer gardens, smoko breaks, or over a cuppa. It's less formal than "chat" and carries a bit of cheek.

Gabba

Definition: Nickname for the Brisbane Cricket Ground (Woolloongabba).

How to Use It: "Heading to the Gabba for the Ashes?" asked Dave. The Gabba isn't just a stadium — it's a Queensland icon. Known for its intimidating pitch, rowdy crowds, and atmosphere, it's where Aussies gather for cricket, AFL, and big events. The word alone conjures sporting pride and local culture.

GAFA

Definition: Acronym for "Great Australian F*** All" — the Outback or remote regions with little around.

How to Use It: "We're off camping in the GAFA this weekend," said Emmett. The phrase pokes fun at Australia's vast, empty spaces. It highlights the isolation and wilderness of inland Australia — endless desert, scrub, and nothingness for hundreds of kilometres. A classic way to laugh at the country's sheer size.

Gander

Definition: To take a look, have a squiz, or glance at something.

How to Use It: "Have a gander at this ute I just bought," said Tom proudly. The word softens the act of looking into something — it's casual, curious, and often carries a hint of shared friendship. You don't "examine," you "gander," especially when showing off new gear or a funny sight.

Garbo

Definition: A garbage collector or bin man.

How to Use It: "Leave the bins out, the garbo comes early Tuesday," reminded Kate. Aussies shorten everything, and this is no exception. Beyond the job, garbo has cultural weight — neighbourhood kids wave to the truck, and it's one of those salt-of-the-earth roles everyone relies on but rarely thanks.

Gee-Whiz

Definition: An old-fashioned exclamation of surprise, wonder, or disbelief.

How to Use It: "Gee-whiz, that storm came out of nowhere," said Nan, peering out the window. The phrase has a retro charm — often used by older Aussies or in a tongue-in-cheek way by younger ones. It softens shock, turning it wholesome rather than harsh.

Tip: Expect it more from grandparents than from tradies.

Get a Wriggle On

Definition: A push to hurry up, move faster, or stop dawdling.

How to Use It: "Get a wriggle on or we'll miss the footy," urged Harry. It's a colourful way to tell someone to get moving without sounding too bossy. Aussies often use it with kids or mates running late — it adds a playful nudge instead of impatience.

Get Nicked

Definition: To be stolen, or as a phrase, "piss off."

How to Use It: "Me bike got nicked last night," groaned Liam. Or, in another sense: "Get nicked, mate, I'm not doing your shift." The versatility makes it handy — it works both for theft and for telling someone off without going full-on rude.

Tip: Context matters — theft vs banter.

Get Rooted!

Definition: A blunt, often angry way of telling someone to get lost — equivalent to "get stuffed" but stronger.

How to Use It: After being cut off in traffic, Dave yelled, "Get rooted!" The phrase is direct, crude, and dripping with Aussie humour. Sometimes it gets misread by non-Aussies as encouragement — but it's definitely not that.

Good On Ya

Definition: A way of saying "well done" or "good for you." It can also be sarcastic.

How to Use It: "Finished the roof job already? Good on ya," said Steve with a grin. Aussies love this phrase because it works as genuine praise or cheeky irony — the tone tells you which.

Tip: A classic Aussie all-rounder. If you're not sure what to say, "good on ya" usually works.

Goon

Definition: Cheap cask wine, often sold in foil bags inside cardboard boxes. A rite of passage for Aussie teens and uni students.

How to Use It: "Spun the goon of fortune and ended up legless," laughed Josh. More than a drink, goon has become a cultural icon — from backyard games (like hanging the bag on a clothesline and spinning it) to budget-friendly pre-drinks before nights out. It represents the laid-back Aussie approach to fun, where price and taste take a back seat to mateship and mischief.

Tip: Expect a hangover. Always.

Greenie

Definition: Slang for an environmentalist or conservationist, sometimes used mockingly.

How to Use It: "Bloody greenies trying to ban plastic bags again," grumbled Dave. Depending on tone, it can be praise or insult — Aussies use it both ways.

Tip: It can be politically loaded — tread carefully outside of jokes.

Grizzle

Definition: To complain or whinge, often at length.

How to Use It: "She's been grizzling all morning about the weather," sighed Baz. Aussies use it when someone's having a drawn-out whine with no real solution in sight — usually background noise more than a real problem.

Tip: Lighter than "whinge" — more about nagging tone than actual seriousness.

Grog

Definition: Alcohol, especially beer. A classic Aussie term for booze in general.

How to Use It: "Pick up some grog for the footy tonight," said Steve. The word is simple, universal, and tied to Aussie pub and party culture. It's one of the country's most enduring slang words.

Grouse

Definition: Fantastic, excellent, or really good.

How to Use It: "That pie was grouse," said Tim after footy training. The word carries a uniquely Aussie warmth — you'll hear it at the pub, the footy, or even from your nan praising your new haircut. Unlike many slang words that fade, "grouse" has lasted through generations, making it one of the few words that both older Aussies and younger ones still share.

Tip: Purely positive — unlike many Aussie terms, it's rarely sarcastic.

Grub

Definition: Food. Also an insult for someone dirty or unpleasant.

How to Use It: "Let's grab some grub at the servo before we hit the road," suggested Sarah. In another sense, "Stop picking your nose, ya grub," shouted Mick at his friend. The double meaning shows the versatility of Aussie slang — one moment it's about a sausage roll, the next it's calling someone out for being gross. In sports commentary, "grub" can also describe a player who plays dirty.

Gunna

Definition: Slang for "going to."

How to Use It: "Was gunna mow the lawn, but cracked a cold one instead," shrugged Baz. It's casual, lazy-sounding, and fits the Aussie love of shortening everything possible.

Tip: Common in speech, less so in writing — unless you're deliberately going Aussie.

Gynie/Gyno

Definition: Short for gynaecologist.

How to Use It: "Booked in with the gyno next week," said Sarah. Though medical in meaning, Aussies often make it sound more casual with the slang, even for serious stuff.

Tip: One of the few slang terms used in both everyday chat and medical contexts.

H

Hack It

Definition: To continue doing something or tolerate a tough situation. It also means to perform or manage a task.

How to Use It: "I don't reckon I can hack it in this industry, but bugger it, I'll give it a shot," sighed Mick. In sport, you'll hear, "The Storm can't hack it this season." It's versatile — used in workplaces, sports, or even just putting up with a long Monday.

Tip: It often carries a tone of resilience — or the opposite, admitting defeat.

Had It

Definition: To be fed up, frustrated, or sick of something.

How to Use It: "Oi, I've had it with youse blokes borrowing my tools and never returning them," snapped Baz. It's often said with finality — the point where patience runs out. In lighter banter, "I've had it" can be followed by a cheeky comeback that softens the blow.

Handle

Definition: A beer glass with a handle, common in pubs.

How to Use It: "Pour me a VB in a handle, thanks, cobber," said Cam. Ordering beer in a handle feels more old-school and pub-traditional than grabbing a stubby or schooner. It's seen as a bit more civilised — even when the bloke drinking it's anything but.

Tip: Regional — more common in some states than others.

Happy as a Bastard on Father's Day

Definition: Sarcastic phrase meaning very unhappy or upset.

How to Use It: "Missed me train and spilled me coffee — happy as a bastard on Father's Day," muttered Dave. The humour is dark, leaning on irony, but it's a colourful way Aussies dramatise a bad mood.

Tip: Definitely informal — it works best among friends who get the humour.

Happy Little Vegemite

Definition: Refers to someone cheerful or content. The phrase comes from a famous 1950s Vegemite TV jingle, which showed kids singing about being "happy little Vegemites."

How to Use It: "Look at the kids, covered in mud but happy little Vegemites," laughed Mum after a long day at the park. In a sarcastic twist, Aussies use it ironically: "Screamin' for McDonald's again? Happy little Vegemite, aren't ya?" The phrase carries nostalgia, as nearly every Aussie grew up hearing or singing the jingle, making it both cultural shorthand for happiness and a cheeky jab when things aren't so rosy.

Hard Yakka

Definition: Hard work. From the Aboriginal word yaga, meaning "work."

How to Use It: "Been on the shovel all day — that's real hard yakka," groaned Mick. It's most often said in physical jobs, but Aussies now use it for exams, projects, or anything exhausting. Saying "all yakka, no pay" is common pub talk when whinging about the boss.

Tip: It's also the name of a famous Aussie workwear brand, so you'll see it on clothes as well as in slang.

Hassle

Definition: To annoy, irritate, or pressure someone.

How to Use It: "Stop hassling me about mowing the lawn, I'll do it later," snapped Pete. Aussies use it in everyday situations — from nagging parents to sales calls. It's softer than outright anger, but it still carries frustration.

Tip: Casual tone — it works better with mates or family than in formal settings.

Heads Up

Definition: A warning or alert to pay attention, usually given before something happens.

How to Use It: "Just a heads up, the boss is coming," whispered Mark as everyone scrambled to look busy. The phrase is handy in all sorts of situations — from warning someone about incoming danger (like a cricket ball flying their way) to simply letting a mate know about a change of plans. In Aussie slang, it's casual, quick, and friendly, showing you're giving someone the courtesy of being prepared.

Hills Hoist

Definition: A rotating clothesline, invented in Australia. A true backyard icon that has become part of the country's suburban identity.

How to Use It: "Kids spent the afternoon swinging on the Hills Hoist," laughed Mum as she pulled in the washing. The Hills Hoist isn't just laundry gear — it's part of Aussie culture. Generations of kids have spun on it until dizzy, dads have pegged footy socks on it after weekend matches, and neighbours have eyed each other's washing from across the fence.

Hit the Nail on the Head

Definition: To be exactly right or accurate.

How to Use It: "When you said footy brings everyone together, you hit the nail on the head," said Sarah. Aussies use it in work, sport, or pub chats whenever someone sums up a situation perfectly.

Tip: One of the few Aussie sayings that overlaps with global English — but often delivered with more bluntness.

Hit the Turps

Definition: To drink alcohol, often on a bender. It comes from turpentine — once used as a slangy comparison for strong grog.

How to Use It: "Haven't seen Mick since Friday; he's been hitting the turps all weekend," laughed Dave. It often implies drinking hard over days, not just a couple of cold ones.

Tip: Suggests excess — usually said half-joking, half-critical.

Homestead

Definition: A farmhouse or main house on a rural property, often surrounded by large amounts of land used for farming or livestock.

How to Use It: "Stayed at me uncle's homestead out bush — fair dinkum, the kitchen's bigger than me whole flat in Sydney," said Tom. In Aussie life, the homestead isn't just a house — it's the hub of farming operations and family gatherings.

Tip: Strongly tied to rural Australia and farming culture.

Hoon

Definition: A reckless driver, usually young, who speeds, burns rubber, or causes trouble on the roads.

How to Use It: "Some hoon was doing circle work in the car park last night," sighed Jenny. The word can sound negative in media or police reports, but in mates' banter, it often carries a mix of criticism and cheeky admiration.

Tip: Widely recognised across Australia — used by both authorities and everyday Aussies.

Hotel

Definition: In Australia, "hotel" often means a pub that also sells food, pokies, and sometimes offers accommodation.

How to Use It: "Meet ya at the hotel for a parma and a pint," said Dave. Unlike overseas, Aussie hotels are central social spots — known for cheap meals, live music, and pokies rooms. A classic example of Aussie English being different — a "hotel" doesn't always mean a place to stay.

Howzat!

Definition: Cricket slang, shouted to appeal for a dismissal. Short for "How's that?"

How to Use It: "Howzat!" bellowed the bowler as the batsman missed. Beyond cricket, Aussies sometimes yell it as a joke when someone gets caught out in daily life — like dropping a pie.

I

I'll Be Stuffed

Definition: An exclamation of shock, disbelief, or surprise. Similar to "I'll be damned."

How to Use It: "I'll be stuffed, mate. Didn't think anything could beat a cold VB on a forty-degree day, but ya proved me wrong," laughed Baz. The phrase captures that Aussie mix of astonishment and humour, often used when something pleasantly unexpected happens.

Icy Pole

Definition: A frozen flavoured ice block on a stick, sold in milk bars and corner shops. Perfect for hot Aussie summers.

How to Use It: "After a day in the sun, I could murder an icy pole," sighed Sarah. Icy poles aren't just a treat — they're childhood nostalgia. Whether it's a Zooper Dooper at school sport carnivals or a milk bar rainbow icy pole, the word taps into Aussie summers and sticky fingers.

Tip: Don't confuse with "ice lolly" (UK) or "popsicle" (US). This one is uniquely Aussie.

Iffy

Definition: Something uncertain, dodgy, or questionable.

How to Use It: "Game started a bit iffy, but the boys pulled through," said Mick. In Aussie slang, "iffy" can soften criticism — instead of calling something rubbish, you call it iffy. It's also handy for describing people or plans that don't quite feel trustworthy.

I Kid You Not

Definition: It means "I'm not joking" or "seriously." Used before sharing something unbelievable.

How to Use It: "I kid you not — saw Harry's missus hook up with seven blokes at Revs," whispered Dan. The phrase underlines sincerity, especially when the story sounds like a Furphy. It's a way of insisting, "this really happened." It's often used to back up tall tales or stitch-ups, so the tone can be playful or deadly serious.

In a Tic

Definition: It means "in a moment" or "very soon." It comes from the ticking sound of a clock.

How to Use It: "Oi Bruce, clean up the dishes," yelled his wife. "In a tic, darl — after this show," Bruce replied. Five hours later, the dishes were still sitting there. Aussies often use it to put things off, sometimes with no real intent to follow through.

Tip: It can mean "right away" or "whenever I get around to it" — context (and tone) makes the difference.

In the Shit

Definition: In big trouble. It could be with the law, the missus, or just life in general.

How to Use It: "Jake reckons he's in the shit with the cops after the last piss-up," muttered Pete. The phrase covers a wide range of messes — from forgetting your anniversary and copping it from the missus to finding yourself in strife with the law. It often carries a tone of grim humour, acknowledging that the situation is bad but also a bit self-inflicted.

In the Tin

Definition: Slang for being in jail or locked up. Sometimes used jokingly when "grounded" by the wife or boss.

How to Use It: "Yeah, nah, I'm in the tin this weekend — missus won't let me out after the pub crawl," sighed Mark. Used literally, it means prison. Figuratively, it's about being stuck under rules or punishment.

I've Had It!

Definition: A fed-up exclamation. Said when someone's reached their limit of patience.

How to Use It: "Alright, youse blokes, I've had it! Stop replacing the VBs in my fridge with toilet paper rolls or I'll go apeshit," yelled Baz. The phrase is a pressure release — the moment frustration boils over into full-on complaining.

Tip: Classic in domestic arguments and pub brawls alike. Tone usually decides whether it's funny or dangerous.

J

Jackaroo

Definition: A young, inexperienced bloke working on a cattle or sheep station, learning the ropes to become a skilled stockman.

How to Use It: "I've only been a jackaroo for a week, and already got bucked off twice," groaned Mick. Jackaroos represent the Aussie tradition of tough, hands-on learning in the bush. It's less about pay and more about earning your stripes.

Tip: Female version = **Jillaroo**. Both terms are still proudly used in rural Australia.

Jack Shit

Definition: Absolutely nothing. Often used to emphasise a lack of knowledge or results.

How to Use It: "You reckon you're a mechanic, but you know jack shit about cars," scoffed Kev. It's blunt and dismissive, but very common in arguments or pub debates.

Tip: It works across generations — one of the more enduring Aussie expressions.

Jaffle Iron

Definition: A sandwich press used to cook toasted sandwiches, especially cheese, tomato, or baked beans.

How to Use It: "Nothing beats a campfire jaffle in the bush," said Dave as he pressed two slices over hot coals. The jaffle iron is more than a cooking tool — it's a slice of Aussie food culture. Families use it on camping trips, around backyard fires, and even at home for quick, hearty feeds. Unlike modern toasters, it crimps the bread edges together, creating a hot pocket of molten filling that's as risky as it is delicious. Part of the fun is checking the iron, hoping for golden perfection, but often ending up with a charred edge or burnt tongue.

Jarmies

Definition: Slang for pyjamas. Often said affectionately, especially by parents or partners.

How to Use It: "Chuck your jarmies on, movie night's starting," said Mum. While some blokes act too tough to say it, the truth is everyone's asked for their jarmies at some point. It can be daggy (uncool) or cute — depends on who's wearing them.

Joey

Definition: A baby kangaroo, usually still living in its mother's pouch.

How to Use It: "Saw a joey peekin' out of the pouch on our walk," said Karen. Joeys are an Aussie symbol of innocence and wildlife — a must-see for tourists and beloved by locals. It can also be used affectionately for kids — "cute as a joey."

Joint

Definition: A place or venue, often a pub, club, or dodgy dive. It can also mean a marijuana cigarette.

How to Use It: "This joint's packed tonight," said Steve as they pushed into the bar. Or, in another sense: "Rolled a joint before the gig." Context makes the meaning clear. The "place" meaning is more common in Aussie English, while the "smoke" reference leans American.

John

Definition: Slang for toilet.

How to Use It: "Back in a sec, just heading to the John," said Luke. Simple, straightforward, and widely understood — especially when you've had a gutful of piss.

Tip: Still common, though younger Aussies might just say "loo."

Jumbuck

Definition: Slang for sheep, especially used in traditional Aussie poetry and song.

How to Use It: "Caught a jumbuck stuck in the fence this morning," said the farmer. The word is iconic thanks to "Waltzing Matilda," the unofficial Aussie anthem.

Tip: Rare in everyday speech now, but deeply tied to Aussie cultural identity.

K

K's

Definition: Short for kilometres. Aussies rarely say the full word, and miles aren't used at all.

How to Use It: "The servo's only a few K's down the road," said Mick. The term is everywhere — from road trips to bush treks. Instead of "kilometres per hour," Aussies often say "K's an hour."

Tip: Visitors should get used to it fast — Australia runs on metric, and "K's" is the go-to shorthand.

Kangaroos Loose in the Top Paddock

Definition: To be silly, dim-witted, or not all there mentally.

How to Use It: "You reckon VB tastes the same as craft beer? You've got a few roos loose in the top paddock," laughed Baz. The imagery is perfect — a paddock is meant to be neat and fenced in, but with kangaroos bouncing around inside, it's chaos, much like someone's thought process. It's cheeky, not cruel, and one of the most colourful Aussie insults.

Kafuffle

Definition: A small scuffle, argument, or commotion that never turns into a full fight.

How to Use It: "There was a bit of a kafuffle at the club over a lighter," laughed Dan. It sounds light-hearted, and that's the point — it's for silly scraps or petty arguments that fizzle out.

Tip: Great pub word — it softens conflict into something almost comical.

Kaput

Definition: Broken, finished, or beyond saving. Borrowed from German, but common in Aussie slang.

How to Use It: "Can't give you a lift, mate — the car's kaput," said Pete. The word pops up most often with old cars, dodgy appliances, or even after a rough day when someone says, "I'm kaput." It works for both things and people, often with a grin.

Keen

Definition: Excited, enthusiastic, or eager.

How to Use It: "Keen for a barbie this arvo?" asked Liam. The word is short and versatile — you can be keen for a night out, keen to help, or keen on someone romantically. If an Aussie says they're "keen," they're locked in.

Keen as Mustard

Definition: Extremely keen or enthusiastic.

How to Use It: "Pub tonight?" — "Keen as mustard, mate." It exaggerates enthusiasm in a very Aussie way — silly, punchy, and memorable. Don't overthink the mustard — the phrase just means "very keen."

Kelpie

Definition: A hardworking Aussie sheepdog, famous for its speed and stamina.

How to Use It: "Got a new kelpie to round up the jumbucks," said the farmer. These dogs are a staple of rural life and often outsmart the stock they herd. Beyond the farm, "like a kelpie" can describe someone with endless energy.

Kero

Definition: Short for kerosene, used as fuel or for lighting fires.

How to Use It: "Grab the kero, we'll get this fire going," said Rob. Beyond its practical use, *kero* shows up in Aussie yarns as the stuff behind cheeky pranks, accidental blazes, or backyard legends. It's got a whiff of mischief — stories of friends nearly singeing their eyebrows or using it in a campfire gone wrong.

Kick In

Definition: To contribute money or effort to something.

How to Use It: "Everyone kick in a tenner and we'll grab a slab," suggested Amelia. The phrase is tied to group culture — whether it's drinks, gifts, or helping a mate. The word is usually used at pubs, barbies, or fundraisers — it's about pitching in together.

Kiwi

Definition: A person from New Zealand. It can be affectionate or teasing, depending on tone.

How to Use It: "Met a Kiwi at the pub last night — top bloke," said Dan. Aussies and Kiwis share a rivalry, but it's mostly playful, especially in sport.

Tip: Neutral word — unlike some nicknames, most New Zealanders happily use it themselves.

Klicks

Definition: Military slang for kilometres, especially in hiking, the bush, or maps.

How to Use It: "The lookout's only a couple of klicks away," said the hiker. It makes distance sound like part of an adventure, not just a number.

It's usually common in outdoor or military circles because it sounds tougher than "K's."

Knock

Definition: To criticise or put something down.

How to Use It: "Don't knock it till you try it," said Baz. The phrase keeps debates cheeky and light — Aussies use it to shut down negativity quickly.

Tip: Great phrase for defending Aussie food or drinks, like Vegemite or VB.

Knock-Off

Definition: Leaving work, or something fake/cheap.

How to Use It: "Knock-off drinks at the pub?" asked Sam, as the clock hit five. For Aussies, knock-off time isn't just leaving work — it's a ritual, often marked by a cold beer with mates. In another sense: "Picked up some knock-off sunnies in Bali." Here, it shifts to mean imitation or fake goods, often cheap but good enough for a laugh. Context makes the meaning crystal clear.

Tip: If you hear "knock-off time," it means freedom — end of the workday.

Knuckle Sandwich

Definition: A punch in the face.

How to Use It: "Keep running your gob and you'll cop a knuckle sandwich," growled the bully. It's an old-school, almost cartoonish way to threaten a fight, often used jokingly these days.

Tip: Sounds tough but rarely serious — mostly pub banter or schoolyard talk.

L

Laid-Back

Definition: Easy-going, relaxed, chilled out — the classic Aussie stereotype.

How to Use It: "He's pretty laid-back about the whole thing," said Ansel after telling his friend he'd been seeing his sister. Aussies pride themselves on being laid-back, whether it's handling stress at work, a backyard mishap, or a blazing forty-degree day. Stubby in hand, feet up, and no wuckin' furries — that's laid-back.

Lair

Definition: A flashy, arrogant show-off, usually young and overdressed.

How to Use It: "Check that lair strutting around in a pink suit," scoffed Dan. Lairs are all about attention — loud shirts, shiny cars, and louder mouths. In Aussie slang, it's not praise — it's mocking.

Tip: If someone says you're "lairing it up," they reckon you're trying way too hard.

Lamington

Definition: A sponge cake dipped in chocolate and rolled in coconut — often filled with cream or jam.

How to Use It: "Want a lamington?" asked Nan, sliding a plate across. Lamingtons are an Aussie classic — turning up at school fairs, Australia Day barbies, and bakeries nationwide. Light, messy, and always best fresh, they've been called the "national cake of Australia."

Larrikin

Definition: A cheeky, mischievous person who doesn't take life too seriously.

How to Use It: "He's a real larrikin — always cracking jokes at work," said Sue. In Aussie culture, being a larrikin isn't an insult — it's affection. A larrikin breaks rules for laughs, stirs people up, and often charms their way out of trouble.

Tip: Famous Aussies like Paul Hogan (Crocodile Dundee) are celebrated larrikins.

Legless

Definition: Extremely drunk, to the point of barely being able to stand.

How to Use It: "After six longnecks, Chris was legless by 8 pm," laughed Mick. The idea is simple — you're so hammered you may as well have no legs. "Legless" is usually funny, not harsh. You can be legless at a wedding, pub, or BBQ, and everyone will just laugh it off.

Lingo

Definition: Slang or language, especially Aussie talk.

How to Use It: "The tourists couldn't understand a word of the local lingo," said Baz. Aussies often laugh about their own slang, which sounds like another language to outsiders.

Tip: If someone says, "You'll pick up the lingo," they mean you'll get used to Aussie slang soon enough.

Lippy

Definition: Short for lipstick, or someone who talks back.

How to Use It: Don't get lippy with your mum," warned Dad. As makeup, it's a casual way to say lipstick — "Chucked on some lippy before heading out." As behaviour, it's about being cheeky, giving smart remarks, or pushing boundaries in conversation.

Lob In

Definition: To drop in or arrive, often uninvited.

How to Use It: "Sorry I'm late, the rellies lobbed in out of nowhere," groaned Kate. In Aussie culture, unannounced visits are both normal and a nuisance.

Tip: Friendly in family settings, but if mates "lob in" too often, it can be a backhanded complaint.

Lollies

Definition: Sweets, candy.

How to Use It: "Grab some lollies from the servo for the road trip," said Mum. It's the universal Aussie word for candy — from milk bars to supermarkets. Parents often use "lollies" as bribes for kids — it's almost a cultural parenting tradition.

Loo

Definition: Toilet.

How to Use It: "Where's the loo? I'm ten beers deep," asked Tom. A simple, polite term that works across Australia.

Lurk

Definition: A shady scheme, scam, or sneaky setup.

How to Use It: "Those blokes have got a lurk going on with fake tickets," whispered Chris. It can mean anything from small-time dodgy deals to serious crime. A very Aussie word for anything that feels suss or underhanded.

M

Maccas

Definition: Slang for McDonald's. The nickname is so widely used that even official McDonald's stores in Australia embrace it on their signage.

How to Use It: "Let's hit the Maccas drive-thru after the footy," grinned Tom. Aussies don't just eat there — it's part of everyday culture, from late-night post-pub feeds to kids' birthday parties. In fact, saying "McDonald's" instead of "Maccas" almost sounds un-Australian.

Tip: It's one of the rare bits of Aussie slang adopted by the brand itself, making it globally recognisable.

Mad as a Cut Snake

Definition: Extremely angry, irrational, or just plain wild. It comes from the idea of a snake lashing out if you try to cut it.

How to Use It: "She was mad as a cut snake when Chris nicked her last beer," said Mick. The phrase isn't only about anger — sometimes it describes eccentric, unpredictable behaviour too. It's colourful, cheeky, and very Aussie in tone.

Magpie

Definition: A black-and-white bird famous for its melodic warble and notorious for swooping during the spring nesting season.

How to Use It: "Watch out, the maggies are swooping near the park," warned Lisa as she strapped ice-cream tubs onto the kids' helmets. Aussies admire magpies for their song but fear them in swooping season — cyclists, joggers, and posties all have their battle scars. Some suburbs track "swoop hotspots" online so locals can plan safer routes.

Make a Blue

Definition: To make a mistake or blunder.

How to Use It: "I made a blue putting fifty bucks on the wrong horse," groaned Dave. The phrase works for everything from losing bets to saying the wrong thing in an argument. It's one of those classic Aussie expressions that softens the sting of failure with humour.

Make a Quid

Definition: To earn money — not necessarily to get rich, just to make enough to get by.

How to Use It: "Old Joe's always looking for ways to make a quid, whether it's mowing lawns or selling firewood," said Baz. It reflects the Aussie spirit of hustling, side jobs, and doing what you can to support the family.

Tip: Still commonly used by older generations, especially in working-class or rural communities.

Malarky

Definition: Nonsense, exaggerated talk, or empty bragging.

How to Use It: "Don't listen to Baz, all that stuff about winning ten grand on the pokies is malarky," laughed Pete. Aussies use it when someone's full of hot air or spinning a tall tale. It can dismiss lies or just playful exaggeration.

Manchester

Definition: In Australia, "Manchester" refers to household linen like sheets, pillowcases, and towels, not the UK city.

How to Use It: "Need to grab some new Manchester for the spare room," said Karen at the shops. The term comes from historical trade links with Manchester, England, which was a textile hub. Aussies kept the word, even long after. Visitors often get confused — you won't find Manchester United jerseys in the "Manchester section" of Aussie stores!

Mate

Definition: The quintessential Aussie word for friend, acquaintance, or even stranger. It can mean warmth, respect, or sometimes sarcasm, depending on tone.

How to Use It: "Cheers for the lift, mate," said Tom. Mate isn't just slang — it's tied to Aussie identity and the idea of "mateship." It can smooth over disagreements, bond strangers, or lighten a sentence. If someone calls you "mate" in a heated voice, it probably doesn't mean friendship.

Mate's Rate

Definition: A discount or special deal given to friends.

How to Use It: "I'll fix your car for you, but only at mate's rates," said the mechanic with a grin. It reflects the Aussie habit of helping out friends while still expecting a bit of cash on the side. It's a gentle way of asking for or offering a favour without making it sound like charity.

Matilda

Definition: Slang for a swag or sleeping bag, made famous by the song "Waltzing Matilda."

How to Use It: "Got your Matilda packed for the camping trip?" asked Jack. It's a nostalgic term tied to Aussie bush culture and folklore. Swagmen in the 1800s often carried their few belongings rolled up in a Matilda. Most Aussies know the term from the song, even if they've never used a swag.

MCG

Definition: Short for the Melbourne Cricket Ground, Australia's largest stadium and "the home of sport."

How to Use It: "Boxing Day at the MCG — nothing better," said Sarah. The MCG is iconic, hosting everything from the AFL Grand Final to international cricket. Mentioning it usually sparks pride in Aussies. Often simply called "the G." If someone says "I'm heading to the G," they mean the MCG.

Melbourne Cup

Definition: Australia's most famous horse race, held on the first Tuesday of November. Known as "the race that stops a nation."

How to Use It: "Put a bet on for the Melbourne Cup?" asked Kelly. Even people who never gamble usually have a flutter that day. Offices run sweepstakes, pubs fill up, and it's almost a national holiday.

Tip: In Victoria, it actually is a public holiday.

Middy

Definition: A 285 ml glass of beer, mainly used in New South Wales and Western Australia. Elsewhere, it might be called a "pot" or "schooner."

How to Use It: "Just a middy for me tonight, got work early," said Dan. It's the go-to word in some states, though interstate travellers often get confused at the bar.

Tip: Know your state's beer sizes — order wrong and you'll out yourself as a tourist fast.

Mongrel

Definition: An insult likening someone to a savage or nasty dog. It can mean mean-spirited, rough, or just scrappy.

How to Use It: "Don't be a mongrel, share the last beer," said Harry. In sport, though, "mongrel" can be positive, describing grit or toughness. A footballer with "mongrel" plays hard and rough. It's one of those words that flips between insult and praise depending on tone.

Mozzie

Definition: Slang for mosquito. Those buzzing pests that ruin summer barbies.

How to Use It: "Can't sleep, mozzies are eating me alive," groaned Ali. They're not just annoying — in northern Australia, they can spread diseases, so the word carries both humour and seriousness.

N

Nah Yeah

Definition: A classic Aussie phrase that actually means yes. The confusion lies in the "yeah, nah" vs "nah, yeah" pattern.

How to Use It: "Nah yeah mate, I'll be there for the footy," nodded Baz. The beauty is in the rhythm — Aussies use it to soften agreement, making it sound more casual.

Tip: Always listen to the last word — that's the real answer.

NBG

Definition: Short for "No Bloody Good." A blunt way to say something is terrible or useless.

How to Use It: "This old ute's NBG, she won't start," sighed Kev. It's quick, sharp, and gets the point across without fluff.

Never Never

Definition: A poetic term for the remote Aussie outback — endless, empty country.

How to Use It: "They've been mustering cattle out in the Never Never," said Jack. It captures the mystique and harshness of inland Australia. Writers and poets often use it to romanticise isolation.

Nick

Definition: Slang for both to steal and the state of something (its condition).

How to Use It: "Car's in good nick — runs like a dream," said Dave, polishing the bonnet. In another sense: "Oi, someone nicked my sunnies at the beach!" Aussies love the versatility — it works as praise ("good nick"), complaint ("bad nick"), or crime ("nicked"). Context decides whether it's theft or condition.

Nick Off

Definition: A polite way of saying go away — the softer cousin of "f*ck off."

How to Use It: "Oi kid, nick off and stop hassling the dog," growled the tradie. It's firm but rarely nasty, often said with humour.

No Worries

Definition: One of Australia's most famous phrases. It means "it's fine," "you're welcome," or "no problem."

How to Use It: "Cheers for the lift." — "No worries." It's easygoing, forgiving, and part of Aussie identity.

No Wukkas

Definition: An even more laid-back version of "no worries." Extra casual.

How to Use It: "Mind if I crash on the couch?" — "No wukkas." It shows total chill — no stress, no fuss.

Noggin

Definition: Your head.

How to Use It: "Watch ya noggin on the ute roof," warned Baz as his friend climbed in. It's light-hearted and can be used in many ways — from "use your noggin" (think smart) to "gave him a whack on the noggin" (took a hit). Aussies love its cheeky, playful tone, so it works just as well with kids as it does in a pub yarn.

Nong

Definition: A fool or an idiot.

How to Use It: "Only a nong would try that jump," muttered Mick. Unlike harsher insults, it can sound almost affectionate among friends.

Not My Bowl of Rice

Definition: Aussie twist on "not my cup of tea." It means something isn't to your taste.

How to Use It: "Country music's not my bowl of rice," said Jess. It's a rare phrase, but it makes sense in multicultural Australia.

Nudie

Definition: Naked. In the buff.

How to Use It: "Kids went for a nudie swim at the dam," chuckled Dad, remembering his own summers. Aussies use it in a playful, harmless way — it's cheeky but not crude. You'll hear about "nudie runs" at schoolies or friends daring each other at footy clubs. It's tied to Aussie humour about stripping off for fun rather than anything risqué.

O

O.S.

Definition: Short for overseas. Commonly used to mean travelling abroad.

How to Use It: "Heading O.S. next month for a cheeky trip to Bali," said Mick. Aussies love to shorten words, so you'll hear O.S. tossed around instead of the full "overseas." Whether it's Europe, Bali, or just New Zealand, saying you've been "O.S." makes you sound a little more worldly.

Ocker

Definition: A stereotypical Aussie, usually working-class, rough around the edges, and speaking with a broad accent.

How to Use It: "He's a bit of an ocker — loud, cursing, and always sinking VBs," laughed Sarah. While some embrace it proudly, others see it as an insult. It's tied to a very "Aussie bloke" identity, often exaggerated in comedy or caricature.

Tip: Use carefully — it can be affectionate or mocking depending on tone.

Off the Beaten Track

Definition: Away from well-known places or routines, often rural or unusual.

How to Use It: "We found this pub off the beaten track — middle of nowhere but best schnitty I've ever had," said Tom. It's not just about travel; it can also mean trying something unusual. The term is often positive, suggesting discovery rather than being lost.

Offsider

Definition: An assistant, sidekick, or person helping out. Common in workplaces, especially in trades.

How to Use It: "Bring your offsider; we'll need an extra pair of hands," said the foreman. The word carries trust — an offsider is someone reliable enough to back you up.

Oi

Definition: The great Aussie attention-grabber. It can mean "hey," "listen," "watch out," or just an enthusiastic cheer.

How to Use It: "Oi! Pass us a snag before they're all gone," yelled Kev. At sporting events, it becomes the iconic chant: "Aussie, Aussie, Aussie!" — "Oi! Oi! Oi!"

Tip: Tone decides everything. Friendly "oi" is fine. Angry "oi" means trouble.

Ol' Cheese / Ol' Man / Oldies

Definition: Slang for Mum (ol' cheese), Dad (ol' man), or parents (the olds).

How to Use It: "Can't come out tonight — the olds are visiting," sighed Mel. Among mates, you might hear: "Ol' man reckons I should mow the lawn before footy." Or, "My ol' cheese still packs me lunch even though I'm twenty!" The terms tie into Aussie humour, poking fun at the generational gap without malice. These aren't formal — you wouldn't use them in front of your actual parents unless you're joking.

On a Good Lurk

Definition: To be onto a good thing, in luck, or having a winning streak.

How to Use It: "Hit the pokies and I'm on a good lurk tonight," said Baz with a grin. It's about catching onto something fortunate and riding it.

On Ya Mate

Definition: Usually sarcastic; meaning "good job" when someone's messed up.

How to Use It: "Forgot the snags for the barbie? On ya, mate," grumbled Steve. At the footy: "Spilled your beer down the front row? On ya, mate!" But in a sincere moment: "Cheers for helping out, on ya mate." This phrase is all about tone. Drawn out and dry? It's sarcastic. Short and warm? It's genuine. Aussies use it to rib their friends, soften mistakes, or share a laugh when something goes wrong.

Op Shop

Definition: Short for "opportunity shop" — thrift shops selling second-hand goods, often for charity.

How to Use It: "Scored this shirt at the op shop for five bucks — bargain!" said Jess. Aussies love op shops for cheap finds and vintage gear.

Tip: Very common slang — every town has at least one.

Open Your Lunch

Definition: To fart, sometimes loudly or unpleasantly.

How to Use It: "Oi, who opened their lunch in the ute?!" yelled Mick. A funny, less direct way of calling out a stink.

Outback

Definition: Remote, inland Australia — dry, hot, and sparsely populated.

How to Use It: "We're driving through the Outback — no servo for 200 k's," said Baz. The Outback looms large in Aussie identity, symbolising toughness, isolation, and adventure.

Tip: Distinct from "the bush," which can mean forest or rural areas closer to towns.

Ow-Ya-Goin?

Definition: Drawled Aussie version of "How are you going?"

How to Use It: "Ow-ya-goin, mate?" asked Bruce as if it were one word. This is classic Aussie lingo — casual, friendly, and said to strangers as easily as friends.

Oz

Definition: Australia.

How to Use It: "Best country in the world, Oz," said Kev proudly. The nickname reflects both national pride and the Aussie love of shortening words.

P

Paddock

Definition: A large fenced area of land used for grazing livestock, often attached to a farm or homestead.

How to Use It: "The sheep are out in the top paddock — need to muster 'em before sundown," said Mick. Beyond farming, Aussies also use "paddock" loosely to describe any open space, whether it's for footy practice, car hooning, or spotting kangaroos. It's central to rural life and part of the country vocabulary.

Tip: City folks might say "field," but in the bush, it's always a paddock.

Para

Definition: Short for paranoid, often linked with being high or overly anxious.

How to Use It: "I'm feeling para, mate — reckon the cops are onto us," whispered Tom after a smoke. The word has expanded beyond stoner circles to mean anyone who's jittery or jumpy for no clear reason.

Parro

Definition: Extremely drunk. Short for "paralytic."

How to Use It: "We hit the pub at noon and by 5 pm I was parro," admitted Chris. The term paints a vivid picture of someone beyond tipsy — staggering, slurring, and usually the life (or shame) of the party.

Tip: Used widely, especially by tradies and footy fans.

Pastie

Definition: A baked pastry filled with vegetables (and sometimes meat), like a cousin of the meat pie.

How to Use It: "Stopped at the servo and grabbed a pastie with sauce," said Kev. They're cheap, filling, and beloved in lunchrooms across regional Australia. While meat pies dominate, the pastie has its loyal fan base, especially among older Aussies.

Tip: Always eaten with tomato sauce — it's practically law.

Pav

Definition: Short for pavlova, a meringue-based dessert topped with cream and fruit.

How to Use It: "Mum's bringing a pav to Christmas lunch," smiled Kate. The pav is iconic in Aussie homes, fiercely debated as Aussie or Kiwi, but always part of festive tables. It's light, sweet, and a source of national pride (and arguments).

Piece of Piss

Definition: Something very easy to do.

How to Use It: "That maths test? Piece of piss," bragged Ben. The phrase is blunt but funny, turning effortlessness into pub-worthy banter. It's one of the most common ways Aussies downplay challenges, from opening a stubby to building a shed. Don't confuse it with an insult — it's always about ease, never about quality.

Piff

Definition: To throw something, often casually or with force.

How to Use It: "Piff us the ball," shouted Mick. Kids grow up using the word on school ovals, and it often sticks through adulthood. It can mean both a friendly toss and a spiteful chuck ("He piffed his phone across the room"). It's a true Aussie-ism — "throw" sounds too formal, but "piff" nails the everyday vibe.

Pigs Arse!

Definition: An exclamation meaning "No way!" or "That's rubbish!"

How to Use It: "You reckon Carlton's gonna win the premiership? Pigs arse!" laughed Kev. It's emphatic, cheeky, and pure Aussie — short, sharp rejection with a grin.

Tip: Stronger than "nah," but not offensive among friends.

Piker

Definition: Someone who leaves early, gives up, or refuses to join in.

How to Use It: "Don't be a piker — stay for one more round," teased Jess as her friend grabbed his coat. Aussies love using this to rib friends who skip a party or won't try something. It's not cruel, just a playful nudge to join in.

Tip: Often said half-jokingly, but it does carry a bit of peer pressure.

Pint

Definition: A large glass of beer (usually 570 ml or twenty fluid ounces), bigger than a pot or middy.

How to Use It: "Make it a pint, none of that middy rubbish," said Baz at the bar. Ordering pints is a mark of seriousness — you're in it for a proper session. Sizes vary by state. In South Australia, a "pint" is only 425 ml, which often confuses travellers.

Piss

Definition: Beer, alcohol, or drinking in general.

How to Use It: "We're on the piss tonight," grinned Mick. The word covers everything: the drink itself, the act of drinking, or the aftermath ("he pissed himself" meaning both drunk or literally wet).

Tip: One of the most versatile Aussie slang words — tone and context make the meaning clear.

Piss Off

Definition: To tell someone to leave, or to irritate/annoy them.

How to Use It: "Piss off, mate, I'm watching the footy," grumbled Kev when his brother blocked the screen. Said playfully, it's banter between friends, but with the right tone, it can be a sharp dismissal.

Piss-Up

Definition: A party or gathering where the main goal is heavy drinking.

How to Use It: "Heading to Dave's for a piss-up — bring a slab," texted Tom. These are legendary Aussie get-togethers, often messy, always involving beer, barbies, and at least one mate making a fool of himself.

Plonk

Definition: Cheap wine, often cask wine or budget bottles.

How to Use It: "Grabbed a box of plonk from Aldi — does the trick," chuckled Sarah. It's everyday booze, not fancy, but tied to backyard BBQs, uni nights, and casual drinking. Don't use it when someone's actually splashed out on a nice bottle — it's strictly for budget booze.

Pokies

Definition: Slot machines, Australia's most addictive form of gambling.

How to Use It: "Chuckin' a twenty in the pokies after work," said Mel. They're everywhere — pubs, clubs, RSLs — and they lure Aussies with flashing lights and free spins. Aussies are notorious gamblers. If you hear "pokies night," it usually means sinking beers while chasing wins.

Pollies

Definition: Short for politicians. Usually said with a mix of sarcasm, distrust, or flat-out frustration.

How to Use It: "The pollies are at it again, promising the world before election day," muttered Dave. The term works for any party or level of government, and is rarely a compliment. Calling someone a "polly" almost always carries a tone of cynicism.

Pommy

Definition: A slang term for an English person.

How to Use It: "The Poms can't handle the Aussie sun — look at that burn!" joked Mick at the beach. It can be light-hearted banter during cricket or rugby seasons, though sometimes it stings. It's often said in jest, but tone matters — use it cheeky with friends, not as an insult.

Pot

Definition: A 285 ml glass of beer, mostly used in Victoria and Queensland.

How to Use It: "I'll grab a pot of Carlton, thanks," said Kev at the bar. The size varies by state, which often confuses visitors.

Tip: If you're travelling around Australia, learn the local beer lingo — ordering a "pot" in Sydney will get you blank stares.

Pozzy

Definition: Short for "position." It can mean a physical spot, or in sports, possession of the ball.

How to Use It: "Found a good pozzy for the fireworks," said Sam. On the footy field: "Mitchell's had forty pozzies today!" It's flexible, casual, and still widely used.

Tip: Everyday slang — from fishing spots to footy stats, "pozzy" fits almost anywhere.

Prezzies / Prezzy

Definition: Slang for presents, usually birthday or Christmas gifts.

How to Use It: "The kids are already tearing into their prezzies," said Mum on Christmas morning. Light and cheerful, it's often used with kids and families.

Pub

Definition: Short for "public house," but in Australia it's much more — a social hub with beer, parmas, pokies, and footy on TV.

How to Use It: "Heading down the pub for a pint and a parma," said Baz. The pub is less about alcohol and more about community and banter. Every Aussie town has a "local pub." Knowing yours is practically a requirement.

Q

Queensland Safety Boots

Definition: A tongue-in-cheek nickname for thongs (flip-flops).

How to Use It: "Chucked on my Queensland safety boots before heading to Bunnings," joked Mick. The phrase is playful irony — highlighting that thongs offer no real safety but are everyday footwear in Queensland and across Australia.

Tip: Classic example of Aussie humour — exaggerating the ordinary into a joke.

Quokka

Definition: A small, friendly marsupial native to Rottnest Island, WA. Famous for its "smiling" face in photos.

How to Use It: "Tourists line up for quokka selfies on Rotto," said Jess. Their approachable nature and cute looks have made them a social media icon, often dubbed "the world's happiest animal."

Tip: Don't touch or feed them — they're protected wildlife, and fines are steep.

Quote

Definition: To give an estimate or price for work, goods, or services.

How to Use It: "The plumber came round to quote on the new bathroom," explained Sarah. In Aussie slang, "quote" often blurs between formal pricing and a rough ballpark figure — tradies especially use it loosely.

Tip: Always check if it's a free quote or a paid inspection — standard practice in Aussie trades.

Quiet as a Mouse

Definition: A common expression meaning completely silent or barely making a sound.

How to Use It: "The kids were quiet as mice once the footy started," laughed Dad. It's often used with a touch of surprise, since quietness isn't the norm in Aussie households. It's a widely used phrase but often said with humour in loud Aussie environments like pubs, BBQs, or family gatherings.

R

Rack Off

Definition: A less aggressive way of saying "piss off" or "get lost." It's firm, but not as harsh as swearing outright.

How to Use It: "Rack off, I'll finish my pint when I'm ready," said Kev, brushing off his mate's nagging. The phrase carries a mix of irritation and humour, so it often softens what could otherwise be a heated moment, making it safe to use around kids or in cheeky banter.

Rag

Definition: It can mean a newspaper, or in older slang, a derogatory term for a woman. The latter is outdated and offensive, so context matters.

How to Use It: "Did you see today's rag? Footy tips are rubbish again," muttered Bill over breakfast. Used in this sense, it's harmless shorthand for a paper.

Tip: Stick to the newspaper meaning — it avoids confusion (and slaps).

Rage

Definition: To party hard, drink heavily, and keep the night rolling.

How to Use It: "We could call it a night, or we could head to Bazza's and rage till sunrise," grinned Tom. The word turns a night out into an all-or-nothing affair, full of chaos and commitment. It's almost always tied to youth culture — if you hear someone over fifty say it, they're joking.

Reckon

Definition: To believe, think, or suppose. A classic Aussie filler word that works in almost any conversation.

How to Use It: "You reckon the footy's still on in this weather?" asked Steve. Used constantly across Australia, it softens opinions, making them sound less forceful. It's almost a national verbal tic — you'll hear it in every conversation, every setting.

Relly / Relo

Definition: Short for relatives. Commonly used when family visits or gatherings are being discussed.

How to Use It: "The relos are coming over for Chrissy, better stock up on beer," said Mick. The word takes the edge off — makes family sound less formal and more casual. It works for all generations but is usually said in a slightly weary or humorous tone.

Ribbing

Definition: Light teasing or joking, usually between mates. It's rarely meant to offend and is often a sign of affection in Aussie banter.

How to Use It: "Forgot to bring the stubby holder? Cop some ribbing for that, mate," laughed Baz. In Australia, ribbing is part of everyday friendships — if your friends don't give you a hard time now and then, they probably don't like you much.

Righto

Definition: It means "alright" or "okay," but often with sarcasm or disbelief.

How to Use It: "Collingwood fans with teeth? Yeah, righto," scoffed Darren. It can show agreement, but more often it's a dry way of calling out nonsense.

Tip: Tone changes everything — with a nod it's agreement, with a smirk it's scepticism.

Rip-Off

Definition: Something overpriced or unfairly expensive.

How to Use It: "Thirty bucks for a burger? What a rip-off," muttered Jake. The term is common in Aussie chats about money, shopping, or travel — and it's one of the strongest complaints you'll hear without swearing.

Ripper

Definition: Fantastic, excellent, top-notch.

How to Use It: "What a ripper day for the beach," said Mel, cracking a cold one. It's pure Aussie positivity, often shouted with excitement at sports, barbies, or big events.

Roo

Definition: Short for kangaroo, one of Australia's best-known animals.

How to Use It: "Nearly hit a roo on the way home — bloody thing jumped outta nowhere," said Dave. Roos are iconic but also road hazards, lawn wreckers, and occasional backyard visitors.

Rollie

Definition: A hand-rolled cigarette made with loose tobacco.

How to Use It: "Oi, got any papers for my rollie?" asked Kev. Rollies are more than just smokes — they're part of Aussie smoking culture. Some see them as cheaper than pre-packed cigarettes, while others like the ritual of rolling, chatting, and sharing around. They often come out at pubs, on worksites during smoko, or at backyard barbies. For many, it's as much about the process as the puff.

Ropeable

Definition: Extremely angry, beyond just "pissed off."

How to Use It: "Spilled my last beer? I'm ropeable," growled Kev. This word sits above "pissed off" on the anger scale. It's the stage where someone is pacing, swearing, and one bad word away from a full-blown blow-up. Aussies often use it when a friend's temper has tipped past ordinary frustration, whether it's over sport, spilled drinks, or life's stitch-ups.

Tip: It's a colourful insult, but still casual. Saying someone's ropeable paints the picture without needing to shout — perfect for storytelling or warnings.

Rort

Definition: A scam, scheme, or dodgy setup.

How to Use It: "Reckon that election was a rort," said Baz over his pint. The word often pops up in politics, betting, or whenever someone feels cheated.

Rubber

Definition: An eraser used to remove pencil marks.

How to Use It: In class, Emma leaned over and asked, "Got a rubber I can borrow?" Her American exchange mate nearly choked before realising she meant an eraser. In Australia, "rubber" is the everyday word for what Americans call an eraser. It can cause a lot of laughs (and confusion) for visitors, since in the US the word usually means a condom.

Tip: Don't panic — in Australia, asking for a rubber in school or at the office is perfectly innocent.

Ruckus

Definition: A noisy disturbance, usually rowdy and disruptive.

How to Use It: "Kids are making a ruckus in the backyard again," sighed Mum. It can apply to parties, arguments, or any loud scene.

Runners

Definition: Sneakers or running shoes.

How to Use It: "Grab ya runners, we're heading for a jog," said Kev. Unlike "sneakers" or "trainers," this word is uniquely Aussie and used by everyone.

S

Salvos

Definition: Short for the Salvation Army, a charitable organisation that runs op shops, shelters, and support programs for Aussies in need.

How to Use It: "Grabbed this jacket from the Salvos for ten bucks," said Rob. Aussies respect the Salvos — whether for cheap second-hand bargains or the work they do helping the disadvantaged. Their op shops are community hubs where donations and thrifty finds keep the cycle going.

Sandgroper

Definition: Slang for someone from Western Australia. It comes from the sandy soil and the burrowing insect called a sandgroper.

How to Use It: "You can tell he's a sandgroper, always going on about Western Australian beaches," laughed Tim. It's a playful nickname tied to state pride.

Sanga

Definition: A sandwich — often a simple one with meat, cheese, or sausage. Sometimes spelled *sanger*.

How to Use It: "Nothing fancy, just a ham and cheese sanga," shrugged Baz. It's the no-fuss Aussie staple, common in lunchboxes, job sites, and barbies.

Scorcher

Definition: A blazing hot day. Very common in Aussie summers.

How to Use It: "Bit of a scorcher today — hit forty-two degrees (about 107°F)," muttered Dean. More than small talk, this word ties to Australia's extreme climate and the shared ritual of surviving summer heat.

Scratchy

Definition: An instant-win lottery ticket you scratch to reveal prizes.

How to Use It: "Nan bought me a scratchy for Chrissie," said Jess. For many Aussies, scratchies are a cheap thrill — a mix of luck, hope, and the familiar disappointment of "one free ticket."

Scrub Up

Definition: To clean yourself up and dress smartly, often for a formal event.

How to Use It: "Look at you — scrubbed up well for once!" teased Mum. It's used half as praise, half as surprise when someone known for thongs and singlets shows up in a suit.

Servo

Definition: A service station — the Aussie pit stop for fuel, snacks, and smokes.

How to Use It: "Pulled into the servo for a pie and a pump of petrol," said Rob. In remote areas, servos are lifelines, doubling as diners, supply stores, and sometimes the only sign of civilisation.

She'll Be Right

Definition: A phrase meaning "it'll be fine," even when it probably won't.

How to Use It: "Left the car unlocked, but she'll be right," shrugged Mick. It embodies Aussie optimism — or laziness — in the face of risk.

Sheila

Definition: Classic Aussie slang for a woman. The counterpart to "bloke."

How to Use It: "She's a good sheila," said Dave warmly. While sometimes outdated, it's still widely recognised as part of Australian identity, especially in older generations.

Shout

Definition: To buy a round of drinks (or food) for others.

How to Use It: "Your shout, mate," said Mick. At Aussie pubs, shouting is an unspoken rule — everyone takes turns, and skipping your round is a social crime.

Show You the Ropes

Definition: To teach someone the basics of a task or job.

How to Use It: "First day on site? No dramas, I'll show ya the ropes," said the foreman. It reflects the Aussie mix of mentoring and mateship at work.

Sick

Definition: Fantastic, excellent.

How to Use It: "That's a sick trick on the board," cheered Dan. While it comes from youth slang, "sick" is now part of everyday Aussie talk for anything impressive.

Sleepout

Definition: A verandah or enclosed outdoor space converted into a bedroom.

How to Use It: "Cousin's crashing in the sleepout," said Mum. Common in older Aussie houses, it's a mix of practicality and nostalgia.

Smoko

Definition: A short break at work, traditionally for a cigarette, now often for coffee or a chat.

How to Use It: "Tools down, smoko time," called the foreman. It's part of Aussie work culture, blending rest with socialising.

Snags

Definition: Aussie shorthand for sausages, especially the kind sizzling on a backyard barbecue. They're cheap, tasty, and practically a national staple.

How to Use It: "Throw a few snags on the barbie, mate, and grab the tomato sauce," called Dave as the smell drifted across the yard.

Tip: A *sausage sizzle* with snags in bread is the backbone of Aussie fundraisers, from school fairs to election day. If you're in Australia, you're never far from a snag.

Spewin'

Definition: Upset or disappointed.

How to Use It: "Missed the gig — spewin'," sighed Kev. The word is short, sharp, and captures that sinking feeling when plans fall apart, your team loses, or the last snag gets taken at the barbie. It's not about rage — it'smore about frustration, regret, or a bit of bad luck. Aussies use it often in sport, gigs, or daily mishaps, so you'll hear it from teenagers to tradies alike.

Spud

Definition: A potato, or a clumsy or useless person (often in sport).

How to Use It: "That player's a total spud," muttered the fan. Harsh but common, especially at footy games.

Spunky

Definition: Stylish, attractive, or fashionable.

How to Use It: "You look spunky in that suit," said Mum proudly. Sometimes old-fashioned, but still heard in Aussie homes.

Station

Definition: An Australian farm, usually very large, often for cattle or sheep.

How to Use It: "Heading back to the station tonight," said the grazier. Stations are a key part of rural Australian identity.

Straya

Definition: Slang pronunciation of Australia.

How to Use It: "Straya, — best country on Earth," said Baz. It's often shouted with pride, sometimes tongue-in-cheek, and usually paired with talk of footy, beer, or BBQs. It captures the Aussie tendency to shorten everything and make it their own.

Strewth

Definition: An exclamation of surprise or disbelief.

How to Use It: "Strewth, that was close!" yelled Kev. It's the sort of word you'd hear in old Aussie films, country pubs, or from your nan when she drops a plate. Like "crikey," it's quaint, colourful, and very Aussie — equal parts genuine and theatrical.

Stuffed

Definition: Tired, broken, full, or annoyed — context decides.

How to Use It: "I'm stuffed after that run," said Rob. The beauty of the word is its flexibility: you can be stuffed from food, stuffed from work, or have a stuffed TV. It's one of those everyday Aussie catch-alls that needs no explanation once you hear it in context.

Sunnies

Definition: Sunglasses.

How to Use It: "Don't forget ya sunnies," said Mum. An everyday essential in Australia's bright climate.

Suss

Definition: Suspicious, or to check something out.

How to Use It: "That deal looks a bit suss," said Kev. Aussies use it to call out something dodgy — from a bloke selling knock-off sunnies to a pub meal that looks past its prime. On the flip side, "to suss something out" means to investigate or figure it out.

T

Ta

Definition: A short and snappy way of saying "thanks."

How to Use It: "Cheers for grabbing me a cuppa, ta," said Jill. It's quick, casual, and often carries a cheeky or sarcastic edge depending on tone. Aussies use it both genuinely and playfully — especially when thanking someone for a less-than-glamorous task.

Tall Poppies

Definition: People who stand out for success, wealth, or fame — sometimes admired, often envied.

How to Use It: "Bit of a tall poppy, that one — can sink ten schooners and still stand," joked Kev. Beyond wealth or status, Aussies often use it to rib friends who show off at the pub or on the footy field. It's half insult, half backhanded compliment.

Tea

Definition: Aussie slang for dinner.

How to Use It: "What's for tea, Mum?" called Jess. In Australia, "tea" doesn't just mean the drink but the evening meal — whether it's meat and three veg, fish and chips, or snags off the barbie. Families across generations still use it daily.

Technicolour Yawn

Definition: A vivid slang term for vomiting.

How to Use It: "Too many tinnies — he's doing the technicolour yawn," groaned Mick. The phrase adds humour to an otherwise grim scene, making it a classic bit of Aussie pub and party slang. It's often used to describe messy nights out.

Tee Up

Definition: To arrange or organise something.

How to Use It: "We've teed up a barbie at Kev's this arvo," said Baz. Aussies use it for everything from casual drinks to formal meetings, and it reflects the laid-back style of getting things sorted without fuss.

Thingo / Thingummy-Bob

Definition: Placeholder words for something whose name you've forgotten.

How to Use It: "Pass us that thingo — the hammer," said Baz. Aussies love these fillers in everyday speech, making them a quirky part of the language when memory fails.

Thongs

Definition: Flip-flops, not underwear.

How to Use It: "Don't forget ya thongs for the beach," said Mum. Every Aussie owns a pair — they're the national footwear of summer, used everywhere from backyard BBQs to petrol stations.

Tip: To avoid awkward moments with Americans, always clarify that you mean footwear, not G-strings.

Throw-Down

Definition: A small beer bottle designed to be downed quickly.

How to Use It: "Pass us a throw-down — I'll finish it in ten," laughed Mick. They're popular at parties or BBQs when the goal is speed over taste.

Tiff

Definition: A minor argument or spat.

How to Use It: "Had a tiff with the missus over the remote," said Dave. Aussies use the word to soften conflict, making it sound less serious than "fight" or "argument." A tiff could be about anything — who left the dunny seat up, who ate the last Tim-Tam, or which footy team is better. Most tiffs fade quickly, patched up with a laugh, a cuppa, or a shared beer.

Tim-Tams

Definition: Iconic chocolate biscuits with cream filling.

How to Use It: "Brew's ready — grab the Tim-Tams," said Mum. They're beloved across the country, especially when eaten via the "Tim-Tam Slam" — using the biscuit as a straw for tea or coffee.

Togs

Definition: Swimwear, bathers.

How to Use It: "Pack ya togs — we're off to the pool," said Mum. Different states use different words (cossies, bathers, swimmers), but "togs" is widely recognised.

Too Easy

Definition: An easy-going way of agreeing to something.

How to Use It: "Can you pick up some snags?" "Too easy, mate." It reflects the Aussie ethos of not making a fuss, even if the task isn't actually easy.

Tool

Definition: An insult for someone arrogant, foolish, or annoying.

How to Use It: "Cut me off in traffic? What a tool," muttered Kev. Unlike harsher insults, "tool" is dismissive rather than aggressive.

Top End

Definition: Northern Australia — Northern Territory, far north QLD, and WA.

How to Use It: "Heading up to the Top End for barra fishing," said Dave. The phrase instantly evokes the wild side of Australia — crocs lurking in rivers, red dirt roads stretching forever, and sunsets that stop you in your tracks. The Top End is not just geography, it's a lifestyle of heat, storms, and untamed country where locals shrug off danger with a grin.

True Blue

Definition: A patriotic term for a genuine Aussie — hardworking, honest, and proud.

How to Use It: "He's a True Blue bloke — always there for his mates," said Kev. It's the highest compliment, tied to values of loyalty, fairness, and looking after your friends. From sporting heroes to everyday battlers, being called True Blue means you embody the heart of Aussie identity. It's often said with pride, especially when Aussies compare themselves to the rest of the world.

Turkey

Definition: A light insult for someone ugly or acting foolishly.

How to Use It: "You look like a right turkey in that hat," laughed Baz. It's less harsh than many insults, often said in jest.

Two-Up

Definition: A traditional Aussie gambling game using coins, famously played on Anzac Day.

How to Use It: "We're off to the pub for Two-Up — it's Anzac Day tradition," said Dave. Two-Up is more than a game — it's history. Diggers played it during World War I, and today Aussies gather every 25th of April to carry on the tradition. Outside of Anzac Day, Two-Up is technically illegal except in casinos, which makes the annual games even more special.

U

Ugg Boots

Definition: Sheepskin boots designed to keep feet warm, once for pilots and surfers, now a global fashion staple.

How to Use It: "Cold morning? Grab your Ugg boots," said Mum. For Aussies, Uggs are comfort first, fashion second. They're worn around the house, at the servo, or even on school runs. Though mocked as "ugly," they've become a symbol of Aussie coziness.

Tip: If you wear them overseas, be ready for Americans or Brits to mistake them as trendy streetwear — Aussies know they're really house slippers.

Uni

Definition: Short for university, where Aussies go after school for degrees — or just for the social life.

How to Use It: "What's next after high school? Uni or work?" asked Gran. In Australia, "going to uni" often means more than study — it's moving out, joining clubs, going to gigs, and drinking goon. The word itself is as common as "school" or "work."

Unit

Definition: A small flat or apartment, often one of many in a block. It can also describe a big bloke.

How to Use It: "Got myself a unit near the beach," said Jess. In housing, it means compact and affordable. But when used about people — "check out that unit" — it's usually describing someone built like a brick wall, not an apartment.

Up Shit Creek

Definition: In serious trouble with no solution, often said "without a paddle."

How to Use It: "Missed the rent payment? Mate, you're up shit creek," sighed Kev. The phrase is blunt and funny — Aussies often soften bad news with humour, and this one is a classic way to describe being royally stuffed.

Ute

Definition: Short for "utility vehicle" — an Aussie favourite, a car with two seats up front and a tray in the back.

How to Use It: "Got myself a new Holden ute," said a proud tradie. The ute is more than transport — it's part of Aussie culture, linked to farmers, builders, and weekend warriors. Even though sales have dipped, it remains a national icon.

Tip: Expect debates between Ford and Holden ute loyalists — friendships have ended over less.

V

VB

Definition: Short for Victoria Bitter, one of Australia's most iconic beers. A classic lager-ale hybrid first brewed in 1854.

How to Use It: "Grab us a slab of VB for the footy," said Kev. For many Aussies, VB isn't just a drink — it's part of national identity. Despite marketing wars with other brands, VB remains tied to pub culture, backyard BBQs, and long summer nights.

Tip: Don't confuse VB with Fosters — locals rarely drink the latter.

Vee Dub

Definition: Slang for Volkswagen, based on the brand's VW logo.

How to Use It: "Check out that Vee Dub, slick ride," said Dan. Aussies often shorten car names for convenience, and Vee Dub has become the go-to for Volkswagens of all shapes — from surf-ready Kombis to city Golfs.

Veg Out

Definition: To relax and do nothing, often involving TV, food, or a cold drink.

How to Use It: "After that shift, I'm ready to veg out with a tinnie," sighed Pete. The phrase reflects the Aussie love of winding down after hard yakka, guilt-free. It's not laziness — it's earned rest.

Vegemite

Definition: A salty, yeast-based spread and a true Aussie staple — though famously polarising.

How to Use It: "Toast without Vegemite? Not Aussie," laughed Mel. For many, it's comfort food, eaten at brekkie with butter. Others can't stand it. Whether loved or hated, Vegemite sparks fierce loyalty and endless debates at kitchen tables nationwide.

Tip: Always spread it thin. Tourists make the mistake of slathering it thick, and regret it instantly.

Veggo

Definition: Slang for vegetarian.

How to Use It: "Got a veggo coming to the barbie — better sort some salad," said Baz. The term is common and not usually offensive, though often tossed around in banter when someone turns down a sausage sanga.

Verbal Diarrhoea

Definition: Talking nonstop nonsense, usually while drunk.

How to Use It: "After his sixth pint, he was spewing verbal diarrhoea," said Kev. The phrase works both as an insult and light-hearted ribbing — perfect for friends who can't stop rambling after a few too many.

Vinnie's

Definition: Slang for St. Vincent de Paul, a charity that runs op shops across Australia.

How to Use It: "Picked up a flannie at Vinnie's — five bucks, bargain," said Rob. Beyond cheap clothes, Vinnie's is part of Aussie culture, offering community support, helping the disadvantaged, and serving as a second-hand treasure trove.

W

WACA

Definition: The Western Australian Cricket Association ground in Perth, known simply as "the WACA." It's a historic venue for both cricket and AFL.

How to Use It: "Heading to the WACA for the Test match," said Mick. The ground has a fierce reputation for its fast, bouncy pitch, making it legendary in cricket circles. It's pronounced as whacker.

Waggin' / Wagging School

Definition: To skip school (or another obligation) and do anything else instead. A classic Aussie rite of passage.

How to Use It: "Shouldn't you be in class?" asked Nan. "Nah, waggin' school," laughed Dave. From hanging out at the shops to sneaking into the movies, wagging is less about rebellion and more about freedom for the day.

Walkabout

Definition: To wander off without a set plan or time of return, usually in the bush or Outback.

How to Use It: "He's gone walkabout again," sighed Kev. The phrase can mean anything from a short stroll to disappearing for days. It carries both Indigenous cultural roots and casual Aussie use.

Walkover

Definition: An easy win, often in sport.

How to Use It: "The grand final was a walkover," muttered Baz. The phrase captures those games where the opposition barely shows up, leaving fans wishing they'd stayed home with a cold one.

Wally

Definition: A fool, an idiot, or someone who is always making bad calls.

How to Use It: "Don't be a wally, that's the wrong train," said Mel. The word softens the sting compared to harsher insults, making it a staple of banter.

"Waltzing Matilda"

Definition: Australia's unofficial anthem, a bush ballad written by Banjo Paterson.

How to Use It: "The crowd broke into 'Waltzing Matilda' after the win," said Rob. The song is more than music — it's a piece of national identity. Sung at sporting events, pubs, and school assemblies, it carries themes of resilience, rebellion, and the underdog spirit that Aussies love to claim as their own.

Wanker

Definition: A crude insult for someone arrogant, selfish, or irritating.

How to Use It: "Cut me off in traffic? What a wanker," snapped Pete. While harsh, it's one of the most enduring Aussie put-downs, aimed at anyone from strangers to mates acting up.

Weekend Warrior

Definition: Someone who only commits to hobbies, fitness, or partying on weekends. It can also mean an army reservist.

How to Use It: "Jim reckons he's a biker, but he's just a weekend warrior," said Mick. The phrase pokes fun at people who go all-in on a lifestyle only when free from Monday–Friday responsibilities. Whether it's motorbikes, gym workouts, camping, or hitting the pub, their dedication rarely extends beyond Saturday and Sunday.

Westie

Definition: A person from Sydney's western suburbs, often stereotyped as rough or working-class.

How to Use It: "Mixing Nike with Adidas? You look like a proper Westie," teased Mel. Sometimes insult, sometimes pride, depending on who says it.

Whacker

Definition: An idiot who talks or acts like nonsense.

How to Use It: "Harry, you sound like a whacker," said Kev. It's dismissive but often light-hearted, perfect for friends spouting rubbish.

Wharfie

Definition: A dockworker, officially called a stevedore. Wharfies are the backbone of Australia's busy ports, loading and unloading ships day and night.

How to Use It: "My uncle's a wharfie down at the port," said Steve. It's tough, physical work that's tied to Australia's maritime history and union culture, with wharfies often seen as salt-of-the-earth workers who keep trade moving.

Whinge

Definition: To complain excessively, usually about trivial stuff.

How to Use It: "Don't whinge, just drink ya beer," said Baz. Aussies love calling out whingers — complaining is fine, but going on and on earns the label.

Willy-Nilly

Definition: To do something without order, plan, or thought.

How to Use It: "He's stacking slabs willy-nilly in the shed," laughed Tom. The phrase adds comic flair to chaotic behaviour.

Wimp

Definition: Someone weak, cowardly, or afraid to try.

How to Use It: "Don't be a wimp, have a crack," urged Rob. Mild as far as insults go, it's often thrown at mates to stir them up.

Wombat

Definition: A slow or simple person, though not always harsh.

How to Use It: "Don't be a wombat, that's the wrong way," said Pete. Wombats are loveable but clumsy — the term reflects that balance of insult and endearment.

Woolies

Definition: Short for Woolworths, one of Australia's biggest supermarket chains.

How to Use It: "Swing by Woolies and grab some snags," said Mum. Almost every Aussie household shops at Woolies, making the nickname universal.

Wowser

Definition: A killjoy, someone who spoils the fun for others.

How to Use It: "Don't be a wowser, have a beer," said Baz. The word has old roots in moral policing, but today it just means buzzkill.

Write-Off

Definition: Something beyond saving — usually a car, but also a plan or a person after a big night.

How to Use It: "That ute's a write-off, Chris," said the mechanic. Equally, "Dave's a write-off after last night" works just as well.

X

XXXX

Definition: Pronounced "Four Ex," this is Queensland's pride beer, brewed in Brisbane since 1924. Recognised by its big red can with four bold Xs, it's a staple at pubs, BBQs, and footy games.

How to Use It: "Long day in the sun? Crack a cold XXXX," said Kev. While VB dominates Victoria, XXXX is the go-to drop in Queensland. It's more than a drink — it's a badge of state loyalty, with ads that lean into humour and mateship. Ordering XXXX outside Queensland can get you friendly ribbing, but in Brisbane, it's almost sacred. The four Xs have become so iconic that the beer is often a cultural shorthand for Queensland itself.

Y

Yabber

Definition: To chat or talk, often excessively. Thought to come from an Aboriginal word for speech.

How to Use It: "The neighbours are still yabbering over the fence — reckon they'll go all night," sighed Harry. Aussies use it for friendly chatter as much as for nagging. It's part of daily life — whether at the pub, around the BBQ, or catching up on the porch.

Yakka

Definition: Slang for work, usually hard work. It comes from the Aboriginal word yaga, meaning "to work."

How to Use It: "That was some serious hard yakka in the sun today," said Rob, cracking a beer. The phrase celebrates grit and effort — whether digging trenches, building fences, or just mowing the lawn on a hot day.

Yank My Chain

Definition: To tease, trick, or mislead someone. Similar to "pulling your leg."

How to Use It: "You reckon Baz caught a fish that big? He's yanking your chain, mate," laughed Steve. It's light-hearted — usually a way to signal tall tales or banter rather than genuine lies.

Yarn

Definition: A story, often exaggerated or spun for entertainment.

How to Use It: "That's a fair yarn, doubt you wrestled a croc," chuckled Nick. Yarning is part of Aussie culture, especially in pubs or around the campfire. Even if it's not true, it's judged on how well it entertains.

Ya Tellin' Me

Definition: A phrase of strong agreement or affirmation.

How to Use It: "Hot as hell today." "Ya tellin' me." Short, sharp, and usually said with a shake of the head or raised eyebrow.

Yeah Nah

Definition: A classic Aussie phrase that actually means no. The trick is in the rhythm — "yeah, nah" softens the rejection, making it less blunt.

How to Use It: "Yeah nah, I don't reckon I'll make it tonight," sighed Chloe, smiling to take the sting out of it.

Tip: Just like with *nah yeah*, the last word carries the real meaning. If it ends in *nah*, it's a no.

You Little Ripper

Definition: An exclamation of delight, excitement, or triumph. It's pure Aussie joy, usually bursting out when something goes spectacularly right.

How to Use It: "The Aussies won in the last over — you little ripper!" roared the crowd. It's high praise and high emotion, usually heard at sporting wins or personal triumphs.

Yobbo

Definition: A loud, rough, uncouth person — usually male.

How to Use It: "The yobbo next door's been shouting at the telly all night," groaned Sue. Though derogatory, it's also used affectionately for rowdy mates who love beers, durries, and chaos.

Yonks

Definition: A very long time.

How to Use It: "Haven't seen Baz in yonks," said Mick. Whether weeks, months, or years, it stretches time in that loose Aussie way.

Yous / Youse

Definition: Unofficial plural for "you." Common in casual speech.

How to Use It: "Yous coming to the pub tonight?" asked Dave. It's not formal, but it's understood everywhere — a marker of working-class and pub slang.

Tip: Avoid in professional settings — it's very informal.

Z

Zebra Crossing

Definition: A pedestrian crossing marked with white stripes on the road, resembling a zebra's pattern. Designed to enhance pedestrian safety.

How to Use It: "Wait at the zebra crossing, the cars will stop," said Mum. In Australia, drivers are legally required to give way, making it one of the safest places to cross. Kids often learn road rules by practising at zebra crossings near schools.

Zest

Definition: Enthusiasm, energy, or eagerness. It can also refer to the citrus peel used for flavour.

How to Use It: "She tackled the new project with real zest," said Rob. In Aussie workplaces, it describes someone who brings energy to the team — whether it's at work, sport, or even cooking a family BBQ.

Zilch

Definition: Nothing. Zero. Complete absence of something.

How to Use It: "Checked the fridge — zilch left but an empty VB can," groaned Baz. It's blunt, casual, and common across Aussie slang, especially when plans or supplies fall through.

Zinc

Definition: Slang for sunscreen, especially the thick, visible kind often smeared on noses at the beach.

How to Use It: "Better slap on some zinc or you'll fry," warned Kev. Iconic in surf culture, zinc isn't just about protection — it's a nostalgic Aussie image of kids with white stripes across their faces in summer.

Zingy

Definition: Lively, energetic, or having a tangy flavour. Often used to describe food, drink, or personalities.

How to Use It: "This mango salsa is bloody zingy," said Sarah at the barbie. In Aussie slang, it stretches beyond food — someone with a quick wit or bright energy might also be called zingy.

Zits

Definition: Pimples.

How to Use It: "Can't come out — got zits all over me dial," moaned Mick. The word is everyday teen slang, but Aussies use "dial" (face) often alongside it, making the phrase sound even more local.

Zonked

Definition: Completely exhausted or out of it from alcohol or drugs.

How to Use It: "After that shift, I was zonked on the couch," said Dave. Among mates, it can also mean being out of your mind at a party, especially on something stronger than beer. The word walks the line between innocent tiredness and wild intoxication.

STORIES BEHIND THE SLANG

Australia isn't just a place on the map — it's a living tapestry of wild history, unforgettable characters, and everyday traditions that have shaped the way Aussies live and speak. From goldfields and bushrangers to pop stars and meat pies, each story adds another layer to the slang you'll find in this book.

These aren't random bits of trivia — they're the backbone of Aussie identity; the legends and larrikins that gave birth to the words, jokes, and cheeky phrases Australians use every day. Understanding these stories helps you know why Aussies say "fair dinkum," why they call soldiers "diggers," and why a simple biscuit can become a national obsession.

AUSTRALIA THROUGH THE AGES

The Gold Rush – When Australia Struck It Rich

Picture Australia in the 1850s: a collection of young British colonies, sparsely populated and rough around the edges. Then everything changed in a flash of gold. When shimmering flakes were discovered in New South Wales in 1851, followed by massive deposits near Ballarat and Bendigo in Victoria, the news spread like wildfire across the globe.

Within months, thousands of hopeful prospectors — known as "diggers" — were streaming in from Britain, America, China, and every corner of the earth. Each carried the same dream: striking it rich with nothing but a pan, a pickaxe, and pure determination.

The transformation was breathtaking. Quiet towns exploded into bustling cities as canvas tents and timber shacks sprouted around the diggings like mushrooms after rain. Melbourne, once a sleepy outpost, suddenly became one of the richest cities in the world, buzzing with wealth, opportunity, and culture. Railways snaked across the landscape, roads carved through the bush, and the young colonies grew wealthy enough to imagine a future beyond Britain's distant penal settlement.

But the rush wasn't all glitter and glory. Life on the goldfields was brutal — cramped tents, knee-deep mud, disease, and backbreaking work from dawn to dusk. Tensions simmered between miners and colonial authorities, especially over the expensive mining licenses that many saw as daylight robbery.

In 1854, that frustration boiled over into open rebellion at the Eureka Stockade in Ballarat. Miners built a wooden barricade, raised their blue flag emblazoned with the Southern Cross, and took up arms against colonial troops. The uprising was crushed within hours, but its legacy burned bright — becoming a symbol of democracy, fair rights, and the Australian spirit of standing up to bullies in fancy uniforms.

The Gold Rush left marks that run deeper than abandoned mine shafts. It brought large Chinese communities whose presence enriched the culture while sparking ugly racial tensions that echo in Australian debates today. It gave birth to slang that's still alive: "diggers," first for miners, later proudly adopted by Australian soldiers in World War I. And it helped forge a national identity built on hard work, defiance, and the sacred belief in a "fair go."

Anzac Day – Where Solemnity Meets Celebration

Every April 25, Australia pauses for one of its most sacred days. Anzac Day began in 1916 to honour the Australian and New Zealand Army Corps (ANZAC), who fought at Gallipoli during World War I. On that Turkish peninsula in 1915, young men from the other side of the world faced brutal conditions, fierce resistance, and devastating losses. The campaign failed militarily, but the courage and mateship of those soldiers carved themselves into both nations' souls.

From those tragic beginnings, Anzac Day has grown into something uniquely Australian — a day that honours all who have served while celebrating the spirit that defines the nation.

At dawn, when the Gallipoli landing is remembered, services are held in cities and tiny country towns alike. People gather in the pre-dawn darkness, candles flicker like stars, and the haunting notes of *The Last Post* carry through the morning air. Veterans march with medals gleaming, families lay wreaths with trembling hands, and for once, the normally casual, joking Aussie spirit becomes solemn and reflective.

But Anzac Day isn't only about grief and remembrance — it also celebrates the lighter side of the Aussie character. During the war, families baked Anzac biscuits using oats, golden syrup, flour, and butter because they could survive long sea voyages without spoiling. Today, kitchens across Australia still fill with their sweet aroma every April, connecting generations to a century-old tradition of love sent from home.

Then there's Two-Up — the larrikin game that soldiers played in muddy trenches with nothing more than two coins and a wooden paddle called a kip. The rules are beautifully simple: coins fly through the air while players bet on heads or tails. On Anzac Day, pubs across Australia legally host Two-Up games, transforming quiet bars into roaring arenas of laughter, shouts, and pure mateship.

It's this balance that makes Anzac Day so perfectly Australian: respect and irreverence, mourning and mateship, silence and celebration. Attend a dawn service and you'll feel the weight of history. Step into a pub later and you'll feel the heartbeat of community.

OUTLAWS, ICONS & EVERYDAY HEROES

Ned Kelly – The Iron Man of Australian Legend

Few figures in Australian history spark debate quite like Ned Kelly. Born in 1854 to an Irish convict family in Victoria, Kelly grew up dirt-poor with a massive chip on his shoulder against authority. By his teens, he was already tangling with the law over horse theft and pub brawls. By his twenties, he and his gang had become bushrangers — outlaws living on the run, robbing banks and playing deadly cat-and-mouse with police.

What transformed Ned Kelly from a common criminal to folk legend was pure theatre. In 1880, during his final showdown with police at Glenrowan, he strode out wearing a homemade suit of iron armour — breastplate, arm guards, and a bucket-like helmet hammered together from plough blades. Bullets bounced off like hail on a tin roof as he fired back, creating a surreal spectacle that burned itself into Australian folklore.

Despite the armour, he was eventually shot in the legs, captured, and later hanged in Melbourne. His final words — "Such is life" — became some of the most quoted in Australian history.

But Ned Kelly became more than an outlaw. For the poor and powerless, he was a symbol of resistance against a system they saw as corrupt and rigged. Kelly himself fuelled this myth through his famous Jerilderie Letter — a fiery manifesto railing against police corruption and demanding justice for ordinary people.

Over 140 years later, his story still divides Australians. His distinctive helmet appears on pub walls, statues, murals, and tattoos. Whether you see him as a cold-blooded killer or a folk hero fighting injustice, Ned Kelly remains one of Australia's most recognisable rebels — a reminder of the nation's complicated relationship with authority and its fascination with characters who refuse to back down.

Steve Irwin – The Crocodile Hunter Who Conquered Hearts

If Ned Kelly embodied Australia's rebellious streak, Steve Irwin captured its wild, passionate heart. Born in 1962, Steve grew up in a world where wrestling crocodiles was just another day at the office. His parents ran a reptile park in Queensland, and young Steve was handling deadly snakes and massive crocodiles almost before he could properly walk.

In the 1990s, Irwin exploded onto television screens worldwide with *The Crocodile Hunter*. Viewers watched in both amazement and terror as he leaped onto crocodiles' backs, wrangled venomous snakes with his bare hands, and shouted his infectious catchcry, "Crikey!" His boundless energy and larger-than-life personality made him an instant global star.

But behind the showmanship was a deadly serious mission: conservation. Steve used his fame to teach the world about protecting wildlife, especially the creatures most people feared or ignored. Whether relocating a problem crocodile or campaigning for endangered species, he lived his message that humans and animals could — and must — coexist.

Together with his American wife Terri, he transformed his family's small reptile park into Australia Zoo, a world-class conservation hub that drew visitors from every continent. Steve wasn't just performing for cameras; he was fighting for the future of Australian wildlife.

Tragically, Steve's life was cut short in 2006 when a stingray's barb pierced his heart while filming on the Great Barrier Reef. The shock reverberated worldwide, but in Australia, it felt deeply personal. For millions of Aussies,

Steve wasn't just a TV star — he was one of their own, a true-blue character who embodied their love of nature, their sense of humour, and their passionate commitment to the things they care about.

His legacy lives on through his wife, Terri, and children, Bindi and Robert, who continue his conservation work and keep his spirit alive on screen. Today, Australia Zoo feels like stepping into Steve's world — his image everywhere, smiling, energetic, and full of life.

Stars of the Screen – From Neighbours to Global Domination

Australia may be geographically isolated, but it has an uncanny knack for producing world-class stars who shine on the biggest stages. What sets them apart isn't just talent — it's that unmistakable streak of Aussie charm, humility, and humour.

Hugh Jackman is perhaps the most versatile of the bunch. To some, he'll forever be Wolverine — the clawed mutant he portrayed across nearly two decades of *X-Men* films. To others, he's the singing, dancing showman of *The Greatest Showman* or the haunted Jean Valjean of *Les Misérables*. What makes Hugh special isn't just his range, but his reputation as one of the genuinely nicest people in Hollywood. Despite global fame, he's remained approachable, down-to-earth, and proudly Australian.

Kylie Minogue started her journey on the humble set of *Neighbours*, playing mechanic Charlene Mitchell. But in the late 1980s, she reinvented herself as a pop princess, and from "Locomotion" to "Can't Get You Out of My Head," she's provided the soundtrack to generations. Australians have cheered every step of her journey, proud that their girl-next-door could conquer charts from London to Los Angeles while keeping that essential Aussie warmth.

Chris Hemsworth followed a similar path from small Aussie TV roles to wielding Thor's hammer in the Marvel universe. Unlike many Hollywood stars who disappear into the LA bubble, Chris chose to stay close to home, living with his family in Byron Bay, where he surfs, trains, and embraces the relaxed Aussie lifestyle. He's become the embodiment of the modern Australian man: fit, funny, and never taking himself too seriously.

Margot Robbie represents the newest generation of Aussie exports. Born in Dalby, Queensland, she went from *Neighbours* (again!) to stealing scenes alongside Leonardo DiCaprio in *The Wolf of Wall Street*. From there, she became Harley Quinn in DC's superhero films and most recently starred in *Barbie*, a role that made her a global cultural phenomenon. Despite her meteoric rise, Margot is admired at home for staying grounded and vocal about her Australian roots.

For Australians, spotting one of their own on the big screen never gets old. Whether it's Wolverine's growl, Thor's thunder, Kylie's pop perfection, or Margot's scene-stealing charisma, Aussies love pointing at the screen and saying, "That's one of ours!" These stars are more than celebrities — they're proof that a country of just 26 million people can make waves across the entire world.

FLAVOURS OF AUSTRALIA

Food in Australia tells the story of a nation — part British tradition, part multicultural innovation, and part pure Aussie invention. Some dishes puzzle outsiders, others have become sacred rituals, but all of them reveal something essential about Australian life and language.

Vegemite – The Taste That Divides the World

Few foods spark more passionate debate than Vegemite. For Australians, it's a childhood cornerstone — spread paper-thin on buttered toast before school, packed into lunch sandwiches, or stirred into savoury recipes. For visitors, that first taste can be a shock: dark, intensely salty, and overwhelmingly strong. But love it or hate it, Vegemite has become one of the most powerful symbols of Australian identity.

The story begins in 1922 when Britain's Marmite supply dried up after World War I. Chemist Cyril Callister was tasked with creating a local alternative using leftover brewer's yeast — essentially beer-making waste. The result was Vegemite: thick, black, salty, and packed with B vitamins.

Initially, Australians weren't convinced. Marmite loyalists stuck with the familiar, and sales crawled. But brilliant marketing saved the day. Doctors and health campaigns promoted Vegemite as a superfood for growing children, claiming it boosted brain power and nerve health. By the 1930s, it was being sold as an everyday essential.

During World War II, the government rationed Vegemite, sending most supplies to soldiers overseas and hospitals at home. That wartime sacrifice gave it a patriotic shine — it wasn't just a spread; it was fuel for the troops defending Australia.

After the war, Vegemite's popularity exploded. The 1950s jingle "We're happy little Vegemites, as bright as bright can be" became embedded in the national consciousness, sung by generations of Australian children.

Today, Vegemite isn't just food — it's a rite of passage. Aussies know the secret: a whisper-thin scrape over butter, never a thick slab like peanut butter. Watching newcomers overload their toast and pull horrified faces has become a national sport.

Tim Tams – Chocolate Perfection and the Art of the Slam

If Vegemite divides opinion, Tim Tams unite it. Launched by Arnott's in 1964, these chocolate-coated biscuits struck the perfect balance of crunch, creamy filling, and melt-in-your-mouth sweetness. Australians now devour hundreds of millions every year.

But the real magic lies in the Tim Tam Slam. Aussies bite off opposite corners, dunk one end in tea or coffee, and use the biscuit like a straw. The hot liquid melts the inside, creating a gooey, chocolatey mess that collapses deliciously in your mouth. It's part dessert, part game, and always ends with laughter — especially when first-timers underestimate how quickly the biscuit disintegrates.

Tim Tams have become Australia's unofficial chocolate ambassador, with visitors often packing suitcases full to take home. The ritual of the Tim Tam Slam has spread globally, but it remains quintessentially Australian — a perfect blend of indulgence and playfulness.

Meat Pies – The Unofficial National Dish

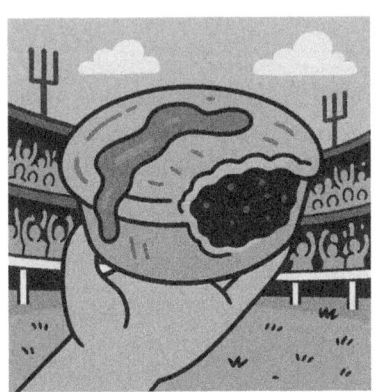

Walk into any Australian bakery, petrol station, or sporting venue, and you'll find them: golden pastry parcels filled with minced beef and gravy, often topped with tomato sauce. Meat pies are so central to Australian culture that they're often called the country's unofficial national dish.

At the footy, grabbing a hot pie with sauce is practically compulsory. The ritual is sacred: hold it carefully to avoid burning your fingers, blow on it to cool the molten filling, and try not to let the sauce drip down your shirt. Australians eat hundreds of millions of pies each year, cementing this humble pastry as more than just food — it's a cultural institution.

The pie represents everything Australians love: it's practical (you can eat it with one hand), unpretentious (available everywhere from fancy bakeries to corner shops), and satisfying (perfect fuel for a day's work or a night at the pub).

Lamingtons – The Sweet Square of Community Spirit

If Vegemite is salty and divisive, and pies are savoury comfort, then Lamingtons are pure Australian nostalgia wrapped in coconut. These humble sponge cake squares, dipped in chocolate and rolled in desiccated coconut — sometimes with cream or jam sandwiched inside — have been winning hearts and covering kitchen counters in coconut flakes for over a century.

The legend goes that they were named after Lord Lamington, Governor of Queensland from 1896 to 1901. The story claims his French chef accidentally dropped sponge cake into chocolate sauce and salvaged the disaster by rolling the mess in coconut. Whether accident or inspiration, the result became an instant classic.

But Lamingtons are more than just dessert — they're community builders. For generations, schools, sports clubs, and community groups have held "Lamington drives," selling boxes of the cakes to raise funds for everything from new playground equipment to footy team uniforms. The sight of volunteers in school halls, carefully dipping squares of sponge and rolling them in coconut, is as Australian as the cake itself.

For many Australians, biting into a Lamington isn't just a sweet treat — it's a flood of memories; school fairs where your mum volunteered at the cake stall; community events where everyone knew the impossible challenge of eating one without coconut falling everywhere. The sticky fingers and the inevitable coconut trail that followed you home.

Today, Lamingtons remain a fixture of Australian life, sold in bakeries, made for special occasions, and still used to bring communities together one coconut-covered square at a time.

MODERN AUSSIE LIFE

From salty spreads to sweet biscuits and flaky pies, Australian food tells a story of practicality, cheekiness, and sharing with mates. But Australia's culture isn't confined to the kitchen. It also shows up in the quirks of everyday life, the traditions you'll spot in pubs and clubs, and the moments when the whole world tunes in to watch Sydney Harbour explode in colour.

Pokies – The Spinning Heart of Aussie Social Life

Walk into almost any pub or club in Australia and you'll hear it before you see it: the electronic chimes, flashing lights, and constant hum of the pokies. Short for "poker machines," these slot machines are far more than games of chance — they're woven into the very fabric of Australian social life.

The scene is uniquely Australian: families gathering in the bistro for schnitzel night or buying raffle tickets for the meat tray, while just one room away, locals try their luck on machines that flash and beep like electronic Christmas trees. It's a curious mix of community and chance that exists nowhere else quite like this.

Australia has one of the highest gambling rates in the world, and pokies are a major reason why. They first appeared in New South Wales clubs in the 1950s and spread across the country like wildfire. By the 1980s and 90s, they weren't just in glitzy casinos but in suburban RSL clubs, sports clubs, and neighbourhood pubs from tiny country towns to inner-city venues.

For many Australians, a flutter on the pokies became casual entertainment — something to do after work with mates, a way to unwind over a beer, or a bit of excitement during dinner at the club. The machines helped fund community facilities, subsidised cheap meals, and supported local sports teams through club profits.

But pokies carry a sharp double edge. While they're part of community culture — linked with fundraising raffles, affordable dining, and club membership perks — they've also sparked fierce debate about addiction and social harm. Critics point to the billions of dollars Australians lose to the machines each year, often by people who can least afford it.

Despite the controversy, pokies remain an unmistakable part of Australian life. Visitors are often surprised to discover whole rooms of them in suburban pubs, right alongside the family dining area and sports bar. It's a uniquely Australian phenomenon that reflects the country's complex relationship with risk, community, and entertainment.

New Year's Eve in Sydney – When Australia Lights Up the World

When the clock ticks towards midnight on December 31, no city on Earth celebrates quite like Sydney. Each year, more than a million people line the harbour foreshore, while over a billion more watch on screens worldwide, as the sky above the Sydney Opera House and Harbour Bridge transforms into a canvas of light and colour. It's Australia's moment to shine on the global stage — literally.

The tradition began modestly in 1976 with a small fireworks display, but by the late 1990s, Sydney's New Year's Eve had evolved into one of the world's most spectacular productions. Today, the event uses around eight tonnes of fireworks, choreographed to music and synchronized with lighting effects that turn the harbour into a theatre of wonder.

At the stroke of midnight, the Harbour Bridge becomes the star performer, releasing cascades of sparks and pyrotechnics in patterns that dance across the water below. The Opera House's iconic shells are illuminated in brilliant colours, while boats packed with revellers bob on the harbour like floating grandstands.

Getting a prime viewing spot requires serious commitment. Sydneysiders and tourists alike camp out from early morning, armed with picnic blankets, eskies full of food and drinks, and enough patience to last the day. Once you claim your patch of grass along the foreshore, you're in for the long haul; but the payoff is witnessing one of the most beautiful celebrations on the planet.

Other Australian cities (Melbourne, Brisbane, Perth, and Adelaide) host their own impressive New Year's events, but Sydney's display remains the crown jewel. For Australians, it's a source of national pride, a dazzling way to welcome the new year, and proof that their laid-back country can put on a world-class show when the moment calls for it.

WRAPPING IT UP – SLANG IN THE BIG PICTURE

From the frenzy of the Gold Rush to the solemnity of Anzac Day, from Ned Kelly's iron armour to Steve Irwin's infectious enthusiasm, from the salty bite of Vegemite to the sweet nostalgia of a Lamington, Australia's history and culture are packed with moments, characters, and traditions that stand out from the crowd. They've shaped not just how Australians live, but how they speak.

Slang doesn't emerge from thin air. It grows from the things people care about: mateship forged in wartime trenches, cheeky humour shared in the pub, wildlife encounters in the backyard, or the simple pleasure of a hot pie at the footy. It reflects the Australian tendency to cut things short, laugh at themselves, and find the lighter side even in serious moments.

When someone says "fair dinkum," "have a cold one," or "back of beyond," they're not just using words — they're drawing on centuries of shared history, culture, and experiences. They're channeling the spirit of gold miners and soldiers, rebels and conservationists, communities that came together over cake sales, and families that gathered around barbecues.

CONCLUSION

Aussie slang is more than just a way of talking — it's a reflection of who Australians are. From the Outback to the suburbs, from the footy field to the local pub, these words and phrases carry stories of history, humour, and a uniquely laid-back spirit.

Some slang terms began with the bush and battlers, while others came from the surf and city life, but together they form a language that unites Australians through cheeky ribbing, mateship, and straight-talking honesty. Whether it's shortening words, adding humour, or turning insults into endearments, Aussie slang keeps communication playful and full of character.

If you've made it this far, you're no longer just a curious reader — you're well on your way to sounding like a true-blue local. You'll know when to say "yeah, nah" or "nah, yeah," how to spot a bogan from a mile away, and even when to chuck a U-ie or call something a ripper.

Slang isn't about getting every word right — it's about understanding the rhythm, the humour, and the culture that sits behind it. And the best way to learn it? Use it. Try it with your mates, drop it into conversation, and don't be afraid to have a laugh at yourself if you muck it up.

So next time someone hands you a snag at a barbie, or you hear a friend yell "You little ripper," you'll know exactly what's going on. More importantly, you'll feel part of the yarn — and that's what Aussie slang is all about.

Thanks for Reading!

I hope you've enjoyed *Australian Slang & Idioms* and had a good laugh along the way while learning how Aussies really speak. My goal in writing this book was to make slang feel fun, easy, and authentic — like having a local mate explain the phrases you'll actually hear in pubs, beaches, and backyards across Australia.

Whether you picked it up for travel, curiosity, or just a love of language, I hope it's given you more than just words. Slang is a window into culture, and now you've got the tools to sound a little more true-blue, to share a laugh, and maybe even surprise an Aussie or two with your lingo.

Your feedback means a lot — not just to me, but to future readers who are curious about learning Aussie English. If you'd like to leave an honest review, please use the QR code below. It helps more people discover the book and keeps this project going strong.

Thank you for choosing *Australian Slang & Idioms*. Keep practicing, keep laughing, and remember — in Australia, there's always time for a gab, a cold one, and a good yarn.

- Lily Koala

Made in the USA
Coppell, TX
07 November 2025

62726527R00094